The Western Isles
of Scotland

A Comprehensive Holiday Guide to

The Western Isles of Scotland

ARLENE SOBEL

NEW ENGLISH LIBRARY
TIMES MIRROR

First published in Great Britain by New English Library in 1972
© Arlene Sobel 1972
Reprinted 1973
All rights reserved

*

NEL Books are published by
New English Library Limited from Barnard's Inn, Holborn, London, E.C.1.
Made and printed in Great Britain by C. Tinling & Co. Ltd., London and Prescot

45001368 5

Contents

Author's Foreword

"The Western Isles," magical islands these are, and mystical as well. Each with its own unique character, its own elements of inspiration. Here are the Hebrides — islands whose seeming isolation off the west coast of Scotland have summoned up fantastic flights of the imagination in the minds of men. Here are islands with haunting names : Skye, Tiree, Islay, Gometra, St. Kilda, Uist, Benbecula, Eriskay, Mingulay and Barra. Here are congenial cliffs and crags, beautiful bays and beaches, magnificent moors and mountains, imposing castles and weather-worn Celtic crosses . . . and so much more. Here you will find the cloisters of Iona, the Cuillin of Skye and the Callanish Standing Stones on the Isle of Lewis, only a few of the spectacles that will delight you and make you dream of ancient days. Here, in the Hebrides, there is peace, escape, romance and enchantment.

Far flung islands will remain precisely that—a distant revery that can never be realized — if no more is given than a little practical guidance. Presently there are available a wide range of books which concentrate in the main on memories of the islands and portraits of its people. While many of these admirable books capture the flavour of the Western Isles, few discuss the difficulties that result from their remoteness, especially those which concern the tourist wishing to holiday there.

This brief book attempts to bring you a little closer to the islands by demonstrating how planning can turn wishful thinking into a never to be forgotten holiday. Subjects such as transport to and between the islands, accommodation, food, day trips, pre-arranged tours and package holidays, places of interest and scenic beauty and sporting areas will be dealt with in as much detail as is possible. The book is aimed primarily at those tourists who like not only a holiday with a difference, but also a holiday with a certain "roughness". For the specialist who is already familiar with the offerings of the islands vis à vis his own particular area, this guide will provide useful information on planning his itinerary and of seeking alternative courses of action.

A book such as this cannot possibly be all things to all people as it would be so diffuse as to have little worth. Therefore I have limited the bulk of the discussion to those islands which are most accessible and which contain the widest variety of facilities and activities for the holidaymaker. However, more than passing mention is made of lesser known (and lesser visited) islands whose unique rewards can be gleaned in a day trip. In either case, the islands offer a great deal of scope for tourists, enthusiasts and specialists alike.

All information contained herein has been checked for accuracy and completeness, although no responsibility can be taken for any possible errors. In as much as the Western Isles are rapidly developing their tourist facilities, it would be wise to personally ensure the correctness of information contained in this guide.

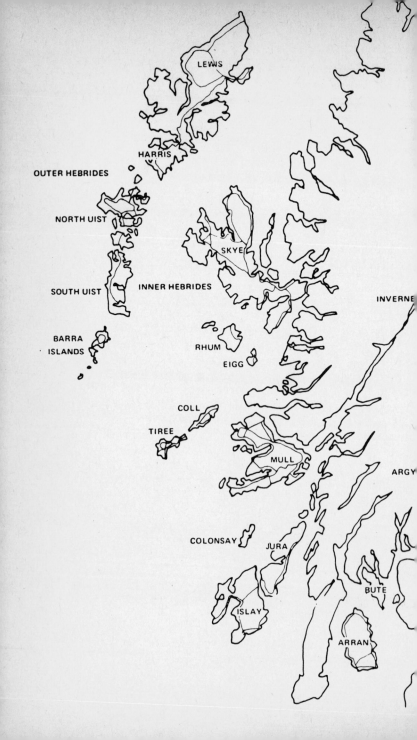

THE ISLANDS

Description

The Western Isles, or Inner and Outer Hebrides, consist of about five hundred islands off the west coast of Scotland (see map on page 12. Approximately one hundred of these are still inhabited, though some only nominally.

Their land mass is fairly considerable (the Inner Hebrides cover 987,800 acres and the Outer Hebrides cover 716,000 acres) but they are said to possess the smallest population per square mile in the British Isles. A number of historical factors, such as the Clearances in the nineteenth century, contributed to their dwindling population, but on the whole it has been their isolation (and the loss of the fishing industry and the consequent unemployment) which has motivated the islanders to move to the mainland. Voluntary evacuation — for example, the removal of the last remaining thirty-six people from St. Kilda in 1930 and, only recently, the departure of the last family living on Scarp — has become an unfortunate necessity.

The main basis of the islanders' economy is crofting (a mixture of small-holding agriculture and fishing), weaving and, for some islands, tourism.

The islands have a varied landscape and on many you will find lochs, glens, gorges, stacs and sheets of cliff rock, heather-covered hills, sandy beaches, stretches of moorland, still salmon and trout streams and awe-inspiring mountains. Birds are plentiful, deer are in evidence and there are a wide variety of flowers and plants.

Winters are usually mild, but the best time to visit is in the summer, then spring and autumn when there is a better chance of sunshine and calm seas.

The day to day language is Gaelic, but virtually everyone also speaks English.

It should be noted that the islanders have strong religious and cultural traditions, and it is appreciated when visitors respect the views on the Sabbath, held in most of the islands.

History

The origin of the name Hebrides is believed to have been derived from Ptolemy's Eboudai which was then Latinised as Hebudes by Pliny and finally corrupted to what we know it as today. Students of Norse, however, maintain that the islands derived their name from the word Hevbredey which pluralised means "Isles on the Edge of the Sea".

In any case what is of much interest here is the composition of the islands. Geologically speaking they are old; as old, perhaps, as three hundred million years, or so the evidence of Lewisian gneiss rock formations demonstrates. Groups of islands have different compositions (igneous gabbro on St. Kilda, the Outer Hebrides and parts of Skye; volcanic basalt on Mull, Canna, Eigg, Staffa and parts of Skye; and meta-morphic quartzite on Jura and the Shiants), and their shape comes from the successive volcanic eruptions of lava (particularly in the south) and the overall effects of the Ice Age. The first inhabitants of the islands arrived *c.* 7000 - 5000 B.C and their Neolithic descendents were probably over-run by the first Celts. The Gael, or Celts of the Bronze Age, entered Britain *c.* 1300 B.C. and colonized Ireland and Alban. The Romans, who invaded Alban in 79 A.D., called the tribe Picts; they eventually ousted the Romans and became the sole nation north of the lowlands until the Scots arrived in the sixth century.

The Scots, a powerful race of Gael, had colonized northern Ireland before the Picts arrived in Alban. When the Romans left the two tribes swarmed over Britain, with the Scots colonizing Argyll *c.* 258 A.D. In 500 A.D. the Scottish King of Irish Dalriada (or Argyll) died. By Celtic law Erc's kingdom was to have gone to his brother, but instead, in 503, Erc's sons entered Argyll and divided the kingdom among themselves. It was united some years later by the one surviving son, Fergus.

Soon the Scots were in conflict with the Highland Picts, the Angles of Lothian and the Britons of Strathclyde. The Scots were Christian, while the Picts and Angles were not. Since the year 400 the Scottish missionaries of both Celtic and Roman Churches had been spreading their religion over the Highlands and Lowlands. In 563 St. Columba and his twelve followers arrived in Iona, established a church and a monastery and then sailed off to convert the people of the Highlands; as we know his mission was successful.

For two hundred and fifty years after St. Columba's death in 597 there was Picto-Scottish strife, and then, in 795, came the Vikings. Around 880, after almost one hundred years of havoc, Harold Fairhair, who had declared himself first king of all Norway, placed the Hebrides under Norse sovereignty. For the next two hundred years the islands were ruled by a succession of warring princes who usually acted independently of the Norwegian crown. In 1093 and 1098 King Magnus Barefoot devastated the Hebrides and forced King Edgar of Scotland to acknowledge his right to them.

In 1156 Somerled arrived on the scene. One of the most famous of warrior chiefs, Somerled was the descendent of Irish kings, and progenitor of Clan Donald of Islay and of the chiefs who, for three hundred years, would be the Lords of the Isles. He and his followers fought Godred, then Norse king of the Isles, and won. He and his successors then held their mainland possessions from the King of Scotland and their islands from the King of Norway. In 1263 Hakon of Norway retook the islands at the battle of Largs, but a storm at sea shattered the Norwegian fleet. Alexander III then seized the Hebrides, which Norway formally ceded in a treaty of 1266.

For the next five hundred years the islands were ruled by Lords of the Isles who made their base on Islay. Through gifts and marriage all the islands of the Hebrides came under Clan Donald sway, with the territory being ruled as a separate kingdom and the clan chiefs being virtual sovereigns in their own right. Iona was granted to vassal clans of two kinds : those of direct Donald descent and those of other names. The Lords of the Isles distrusted the Scottish kings as they had introduced the feudal system into their kingdom. Flouting authority, they staged a number of rebellions. In 1493 James the Fourth brought John the Second, the ninth chief of the house of Islay and fourth Lord of the Isles, to trial and his lands and titles were declared forfeit. James then granted royal charters to the chief land-holders.

For the next century the various clans warred against each other, each vying to be supreme head. In 1609 James the Sixth sent Lord Ochiltree to the Isles where he seized the castles of Mull and, soon after, captured all the chiefs. They were released on the ratification of the nine statutes at a council on Iona, which signalled the end to clan feuding. The Campbells of Argyll were then given Islay and Kintyre as a reward for services to the crown and treacheries to neighbours.

In 1745 Prince Charles Edward (Bonnie Prince Charlie) landed on Eriskay. The clans then rose for their last great rebellion against the crown, which was crushed at Culloden a year later. The clansmen were disarmed and the chiefs' heritable jurisdiction was abolished, thenceforward transforming them to landlords and their clansmen to tenants.

For a while the islanders enjoyed a brief prosperity, but in the end the social upheaval of the destruction of the clan system forced them into a precarious position. The increase in population meant that the crofts were divided into smaller and smaller holdings. There was no security of tenure as the land was owned by a "laird" or held on long lease, with the crofter owing rent and services. Sheep farming began to predominate over cattle farming, with both the cattle and the surplus population being brought to the mainland, against their will. The nineteenth century was therefore marked by Clearances, and from 1842 there was a steady drain of population which, in spite of all efforts, is still going on until this day. In 1843 the Free Church emerged with missionary fervour to recapture the islands, and all were converted except for Barra and South Uist which remained Catholic.

For the next thirty years or so the islanders were rack-rented by absentee landlords and their land was impoverished by the sheep who cropped the grass too short. In 1882 the crofters rioted and warships had to be sent to Skye to quell them. A report by a Royal Commission resulted in the Crofter's Holding Act of 1886 which gave the crofters security of tenure, grants for improvements and a fair rent. The "black houses" which once sheltered the crofter and his animals were gradually replaced by "white houses", mostly built by the crofters themselves and later aided by loans and grants. Modern amenities have only recently been introduced.

During the First World War the islanders lost many of their men. When the survivors returned home many were provoked by their lack of land, and this resulted in land-raiding and squatting. The Department of Agriculture and the Land Courts then bought more land for new crofts and for the enlargement of old crofts. Fishing, as an industry, also shrank because of poaching, the closing of European markets and the dumping of cheap Norwegian herring.

In recent years attempts have been made to salvage the fishing industry. The government contributed a dozen fishing boats to an Outer Isles Fishery Training Scheme, and the Minch, which separates the Inner from the Outer Hebrides, was closed to foreign trawlers. Poaching still continues on the eastern shores.

Crofters, too, have been aided by further subsidies and the advice of experts. Unfortunately only a few holdings are large enough to be economically viable. At present many islanders subsist on the money gained from subsidiary industries such as tweed-weaving and lobster, prawn and herring fishing. Additional work has been offered on the revived seaweed industry and on the roads and, on some of the Inner Isles, in distilleries and by afforestation work. Grass is being re-seeded and cattle rearing has begun again. There has been a sudden upsurge in tourism. It is to be hoped that prosperity may now be regained ...

How to get there

We have used the words "remote" and "isolated" to describe the Western Isles, and this is true — to a point. The islands are in fact accessible, though some are more so than others. For this reason careful consideration should be given to the following, especially to those of you who are planning a more intricate holiday of "island hopping". All routes and schedules must be re-checked before your departure as new or altered services come into operation often quite suddenly. In addition, off-peak and winter services vary considerably from those of the summer, and for this reason you should consult those particular timetables.

Primarily the three points of departure *by sea* to the Western Isle are Kyle of Lochalsh, Mallaig and Oban; Fort William is a fourth point but it services only Iona by way of Oban. The fifth point is Tarbert, Kennacraig (Loch Fyne) and from here you can sail to Islay, Jura, Colonsay and Gigha.

These ports may be reached with some ease by public and private transport.

British Rail, solely and in conjunction with Highland Omnibuses Ltd.; Western SMT Co. Ltd.; W. Alexander Ltd.; Scottish Omnibuses Ltd.; David MacBrayne Ltd. and Caledonian Steam Packet Co. Ltd., offer a number of services to suit your individual needs.

The first is British Rail's Motorail service by which you, your family, your car, luggage, boat and dog are transported by (overnight) train to a Motorail terminal to Inverness, Edinburgh or Perth, and from there you can drive to Kyle, Mallaig or Oban. The Motorail is especially good for those travellers who wish to take their cars but who want to save their time and energy on the first leg of their trip. In addition, Motorail can also save you some money as it offers a 10% discount on room rates in BTH hotels. Prices, schedules, conditions and booking forms are available at any British Rail Station, Travel Office or Appointed Travel Agent.

Another means of transport is purely public. Eight days of unlimited travel throughout the Highlands and Islands can be got for a reasonable cost with the purchase of the Highlands and Islands Development Board's new Travelpass. The Travelpass is recommended for those people who wish to make a speedy circuit of the region without the use of a car and with minimum expenditure. During the summer months, a Travelpass costs £14.50 (children £9.00); during the spring and autumn it costs two pounds less for adults and one pound less for children. These prices refer to 1972 and will no doubt be revised in 1973 when an extended and improved Travelpass service will come into operation. Further information can be

18

obtained from Highlands and Islands Travelpass, 25 Queens-gate, Inverness.

Once you have arrived at the aforementioned ports, you will be in the hands (some say at the mercy) of David MacBraynes or, at times, the Caledonian Steam Packet Co. and Western Ferries Ltd. MacBraynes have almost completely monopolised transport (both steamer and bus) to, on and between the islands. What MacBraynes do offer is scope, both for tourists who have come with or without their cars or caravans. For those in the former case, transport is, admittedly, much easier as tourists will merely have to heed with care the timetables of sea voyages. For those "on foot" there are some difficulties, though these are surmountable. Planning is paramount here — and this is no mean feat. Boat and bus schedules quite often do not co-ordinate and the trick is how to prevent yourself from being stranded in a place against your will. The very hardy can "foot it"; the less hardy can take a taxi, but these are few and far between (ask the local Tourist Office) and very expensive. Hitch-hiking would be simple if there was traffic, but on the islands of the Outer Hebrides there isn't. Tour bus drivers — and I can attest to this from personal experience — can be very kind to the stranded . . . but keep this under your rucksack or case.

To return to MacBraynes : their full name and address is David MacBrayne Ltd., Travel Centre, 302 Buchanan Street, Glasgow G1 2NQ. On request they will send you their time-table of sailings, and a very clear timetable it is. (Drivers take note of the Car 'Rover' Tickets.) Eighteen different voyages are offered — some car ferry and some steamer — to ports in Lewis, Harris, North Uist, South Uist, Barra, Skye, Raasay, Canna, Muck, Eigg, Coll, Tiree, Mull, Iona and Staffa (the last without stopping). Additionally MacBraynes offer a number of day excursions from Oban, Fort William, Tobermory (on Mull), Craignure (on Mull), Portree and Uig (on Skye), Inverness, Mallaig and the Kyle of Lochalsh. Prices, conditions and booking forms are included in the timetable, along with an excellent map of their services, a table of sunshine hours and a listing of Highland events.

It is also possible to fly to the islands via British European Airways and Loganair (the latter have a Sunday service), Peregrine Air Service do charters. Almost all flights are from Glasgow Airport, Abbotsinch; a few are from Dalcross Airport, Inverness. There are airports located in Stornoway (Lewis), Balivanich (Benbecula and from thence to North and South Uist by hired car and bus), Northbay (Barra), Scarinish (Tiree), Port Ellen (Islay and from thence to Jura by hired car and ferry). Prices, schedules and booking forms can be obtained from British European Airways, Dorland Hall, Lower Regent Street, London, W.1.; Loganair, Glasgow Airport, Abbotsinch; Peregrine Air Services, Dalcross Airport, Inverness.

The above cover main services and are only given as suggestions. Reaching the islands will depend greatly on where you are coming from, what type of transport you intend to use and how much money you plan to spend on your holiday. The last point is important : sailing from island to island for an entire family can be quite expensive, especially if you have a car or caravan. Do take this into account; I sincerely hope it will not deter you.

Inter- and intra-island travel

We have mentioned that MacBraynes run the majority of the scheduled sailings to and between the islands. However, fishermen or boat owners are also willing to take you from island A to island B, for a price, of course. These gentlemen charge according to "the head" and the more people they can fit on their boats, the less you will have to pay. They are very able and even short runs can be an adventure. Local Tourist Offices (their names and addresses will be supplied under the individual listings) can arrange transport, even on the spur of the moment. You can also "book" in advance, though in both cases the sailings are subject to the tides.

Intra-island travel is, of course, quite simple if you have a car, caravan and some maps. For those who must rely on public transport let it be said that services are limited. Be sure to obtain bus schedules from the local Tourist Office beforehand and re-check it on your arrival on the islands. Fortunately, if all else fails, you can hire a car (ask the Tourist Office for a list of car-hirers).

Accommodation

It has been mentioned that some islands are presently in the birth throes of tourism and hence they suffer from those difficulties. This is especially true with respect to accommodation. On Skye, an island which has catered to a large influx of tourists, and on Lewis and Mull more sophisticated accommodation is available and much sought after. Booking far in advance is strongly recommended. On other islands there are guest houses and bed and breakfast places (many with evening meals as eating facilities are scarce) and listings of these are provided by the local Tourist Office on each island or from the Tourist Offices in Inverness, Kyle of Lochalsh, Oban, Mallaig and Fort William, to name a few.

A number of the islanders will rent out their homes during the summer months, and these range from the primitive to the palatial. The latter are often advertised in *The Times* (daily and Sunday) and are well worth their price if you are going with other families. Local Tourist Offices also have complete listings of these.

Cottages may also be rented but for something a little more basic there are youth hostels, located on Skye, Raasay, Mull, Harris, and Uist. For membership and details write to The Scottish Youth Hostels Association, 7 Glebe Crescent, Stirling. Camp and caravan sites are much in evidence throughout the Western Isles. Further information and membership applications can be obtained from The Camping Club of Great Britain and Ireland Ltd., 11 Lower Grosvenor Place, London, S.W.1 and the Caravan Club, 65 South Molton Street, London W1Y 2AB.

Eating facilities

As with accommodation, eating facilities are largely dependent on the sophistication vis à vis tourism on the individual
islands. Restaurants and cafes are fairly abundant in such
large centres as Portree (Skye), Stornoway (Lewis), Tarbert
(Harris), Tobermory (Mull) and so on but there are few (if
any) in some of the lesser tourist spots. Campers and caravan-
ers can purchase food on the mainland and transport it to the
islands; additional supplies can be bought in the local stores
or from the mobile shops. Some hostels provide facilities but
many do not; it is therefore recommended that you purchase
ahead or procure on the spot. Again, many of the hotels,
guest houses and bed and breakfast places provide evening
meals. Pubs are not particularly abundant.

What to wear

Generally speaking temperatures are moderate : it is warm in
the summer sun, although it does get cooler in the evenings.
Heavy clothing should be brought and worn on the sailings
as the wind can be rather bracing. Additionally you should
supply yourself with a good mac and strong shoes, and of
course, all clothing suitable for the various sports.

Alternative holidays

As you can see from the preceding the Western Isles provide
numerous outlets for a variety of different types of holidays.
The majority require a little more effort than you would
ordinarily make but the rewards are equal if not greater.
Everything depends on what you want to make of your
holiday and where your interests lie. This is not to say that
three weeks in a good hotel on Skye is better than three weeks
of camping in the Outer Hebrides or three weeks spent in a
derelict house on a deserted island such as Eilean on Tighe

(in the Shiants) — not at all, in fact. The Western Isles, in a sense, bring out the individual and personal in you and hence the choice (and value) of one holiday over the next is simply relative.

There are alternatives, however, and these should be borne in mind. Day-trips aside (these can be easily arranged by Travel Agents in Fort William), there are many opportunities available to those of you who wish to spend your entire holiday on the islands. The Highlands and Islands Development Board have organised some splendid package holidays to the islands, aimed particularly at those with special sporting or outdoor interests.. All holidays vary in price, length of stay, amenities, conditions, season and sporting facilities — so much so, in fact, that a complete listing should be obtained to make your choice. Inclusive holidays will be offered but mainly for sports and special activities. Write to : The Highlands and Islands Development Board, Inverness, or ask at your local A.B.T.A. Travel Agent.

Courses covering sailing, canoeing, climbing, hillwalking, camping, map reading, elementary marine biology, basic geology, outdoor survival techniques, trout, sea and lobster fishing and an expedition to the Handa Island Bird Reserve are given at The John Ridgway School of Adventure at Rhiconich. For more information write to Captain John Ridgway, M.B.E., Ardmore, Rhiconich, by Lairg, Sutherland. The National Trust for Scotland (5 Charlotte Square, Edinburgh EH2 4DU) has organized a truly adventurous holiday called the St. Kilda Cruise, one of which lands a small "working party" on the island. Further details can be obtained from the above (also see chapter on St. Kilda).

Again, the above "packages" are merely suggestions and they do not cover all of the possibilities for all-inclusive holidays in the Western Isles. Your local Travel Agent may prove helpful in suggesting other holidays of this nature.

Sport

The Western Isles do not, as yet, cater very much to those engaged in field sports; however, The Highlands and Islands Development Board is presently working on improving this area.

There is plenty of scope for anglers, with some good trout, sea trout and salmon fishing on a variety of islands (see individual listings). It is recommended that you purchase and/or consult "Scotland for Fishing" and "Scotland for Sea Angling" (available from The Scottish Tourist Board, 2 Rutland Place, Edinburgh EH1 2YU; price 25p and 20p) and "Where to Fish" (price £2.30) for information on laws and licences.

Some of the islands are particularly noteworthy for climbing and hillwalking; again these will be found under the separate listings for each island.

Other outdoor activities include golf, pony trekking, tennis, rambling and cycling.

Places of interest

The Western Isles are quite rich in the historical and the legendary and visitors will find many places to visit, including historical, archæological and religious sites. Specific information will be given in the text.

Specialised interests

Ornithologists often rub shoulders with botanists, photographers with zoologists, mammalogists with archæologists, ecclesiologists with geologists, painters with ... the list is extensive ... Specialists (and enthusiasts) will discover abundant resources in the Western Isles for their particular interests. Those people who thought they simply came "for the scenery" will certainly find an awakening of a certain deeper curiosity: the Western Isles have a way of doing this, almost in opposition to one's will.

A note to the reader

Although nightlife isn't exactly lacking on the islands, it isn't what they're all about. Nor are the islands a buyer's paradise, except, perhaps, for a few local crafts and, of course, Harris Tweed. It is true that throughout the summer months there are numerous "events" — cattle and flower shows, Highland games, golf weeks and gala weeks, angling contests, regattas and ceilidhs — and undoubtedly these are very entertaining. One can say, however, that the Western Isles are the last remote outpost in the British Isles. Tranquillity and peace are what they offer, and you should go there with a view towards this . . .

Further information

The scope of this guide is limited to those salient points of interest to those wishing to holiday in the Western Isles. It is only possible to touch on these and therefore the reader is directed to other sources from which they can glean more detailed information. A number of the following sources have been mentioned in the text; here I will gather them together and add still others to the list.

The Scottish Tourist Board, 2 Rutland Place, Edinburgh EH1 2YU.

The Highlands and Islands Development Board, Bridge House, Bank Street, Inverness.

British Tourist Authority, 239 Old Marylebone Road, London, N.W.1

British Travel Association, 64 St. James's Street, London, S.W.1.

David MacBrayne Ltd., Travel Centre, 302 Buchanan Street, Glasgow G1 2NQ.

Caledonian Steam Packet Co. Ltd., Kyle of Lochalsh.

Western Ferries, Ltd., Kennacraig, Tarbert (Loch Fyne), Argyll.

British Rail, Travel Centre, Regent Street, London, S.W.1.

British European Airways, Dorland Hall, Lower Regent Street, London, S.W.1.

Loganair, Glasgow Airport, Abbotsinch.

Peregrine Air Service, Dalcross Airport, Inverness.

Highlands and Islands Travelpass, 25 Queensgate, Inverness.

The Scottish Youth Hostels Association, 7 Glebe Crescent, Stirling.

The Camping Club of Great Britain and Ireland, Ltd., 11 Lower Grosvenor Place, London, S.W.1.

The Caravan Club, 65 South Molton Street, London, W1Y 2AB.

Fort William and District Tourist Organisation, Fort William, Inverness-shire.

Oban, Mull and Dist. Tourist Organisation, Albany St., Oban

Mallaig Tourist Organisation, Mallaig, Inverness-shire.

Kyle of Lochalsh Tourist Organisation, Kyle of Lochalsh, Inverness-shire.

Inverness and Loch Ness Tourist Organisation, 2 Academy Street, Inverness.

Mid-Argyll, Kintyre and Islay Tourist Organisation, Campbeltown, Argyllshire.

Sutherland Tourist Organisation, The Square, Durnoch, Sutherland.

Wester Ross Tourist Organisation, Sands Estate, Gairloch, Wester Ross.

Ness Travel Ltd., 14 Union Street, Inverness.

Captain John Ridgway, M.B.E., Ardmore, Rhiconich, by Lairg, Sutherland.

The National Trust for Scotland, 5 Charlotte Square, Edinburgh EH2 4DU.

The Nature Conservancy, 12 Hope Terrace, Edinburgh EH9 2AS.

The Forestry Commission, 25 Drumsheugh Gnds., Edinburgh 3.

The Countryside Commission for Scotland, Branklyn, Dundee Road, Perth.

The Royal Society for the Protection of Birds, 17 Regent Terrace, Edinburgh EH7 5BN.

The Ramblers Association, 1/4 Crawford Mews, London, W.1.

British Field Sports Society, Haig House, 23 Drumsheugh Gardens, Edinburgh 1.

The Royal Automobile Club, Scottish Western Counties Office, 242 West George Street, Glasgow G2 4QZ.
The Automobile Association, Argos House, 269 Argyle Street, Glasgow C1.

Local information

The first entry in each Local Information section of this guide gives the address of the local Tourist Office on each island or of a Tourist Office on the mainland which will supply additional information.

These offices will be pleased to furnish you with both gratis literature and literature for which there is a nominal charge (the latter is well worth the price). They will also supply you with details concerning banks, early-closing days, car and caravan hirers and repairers, places of worship, and locations of doctors and/or hospitals.

Bibliography

There are scores of books devoted to the Western Isles, each with its particular orientation. The majority, however, are of the type mentioned in the Foreword : memories of the islands and portraits of its people. A few of these might be worth perusing, but by no means is the following list a complete one.

A JOURNAL OF A TOUR TO THE HEBRIDES WITH SAMUEL JOHNSON, James Boswell.

A TANGLE OF ISLANDS, L. R. Higgins.

THE ENCHANTED ISLES : Hebridean Portraits and Memories, Alasdair Alpin MacGregor.

THE CHARM OF SCOTLAND, John Herries McCulloch.

IN SEARCH OF SCOTLAND, H. V. Morton.

THE HEBRIDES, W. H. Murray.

THE HIGHLANDS AND ISLANDS OF SCOTLAND, A. C. O'Dell and K. Walton.

THE INNER HEBRIDES AND THEIR LEGENDS; THE OUTER HEBRIDES AND THEIR LEGENDS; SKYE : THE ISLAND AND ITS LEGENDS, Otta F. Swire.

THE LIFE AND DEATH OF ST. KILDA, Tom Steel.

THE INNER HEBRIDES

SKYE

Description

The nearest island to the mainland and the largest of the Inner Isles is the Isle of Skye, long heralded as "the gem of the Western seas".

It is, indeed, a magical place where sun, cloud and mist work daily miracles upon its magnificent mountains and mysterious lochs. Here history and legend — romance, as well — combine to cast an aura of charm that draws the visitor back, time and again.

Scenically Skye is remarkably varied and has perhaps more to offer the tourist than any other area of equal size in the British Isles. Of emotional attachments it has many, and its residents can almost assure you that your stay on Skye — however brief it may be — will remain the most vivid of your holiday memories.

The derivation of its name has long been in dispute. In Gaelic, Skye has been called "the Isle of Mist", and, to be sure it appears that way to the onlooker. However, many authorities have interpreted the meaning of the name through the word "sgiath" or "wing" in Gaelic. A brief glance at the map of Scotland bears this out : Skye is "attached" to the mainland by the tapered straits which extend from its base to its tips, in the form of the peninsulas of Trotternish and Vaternish, into the surging waters of the Minch.

Travelling around the island is quite easy as the island is very manageable : it is forty-eight miles long and twelve miles broad. The coastline runs for three hundred miles, and no part of the island is more than five miles from the sea.

Most tourists visit Skye during the months of July and August and at that time the island seems to rouse itself from its dreamy sleep and become a bustling place. May and June are also recommended as during these months there are long hours of daylight and a great deal of sunshine. Autumn is also a good time to visit as on Skye the changing colours are particularly brilliant.

The total population of Skye is presently a bit under eight thousand and, unlike many of the other islands, it has not in recent years fallen prey to de-population.

All the names are Norse and Gaelic. In remote ages it was Viking territory. The Norsemen colonized the island and many of its children have the pale hair and the blue eyes of their ancestors. The hills, the lochs and many of the peaks were named by the Vikings and, as H. V. Morton has so aptly written, "even now the shadow of (their) long (boats) falls across the craggy estuaries, and the ghost of Thor surely walks the Sgurr nan Gillean when the lightning cracks from peak to peak and the thunder rolls and rocks from Alasdair to Dearg".

The heart of this gem is the Cuillin or the Coolins, the most mighty mountain range in Britain. Jagged, irregular and affording a variety of beautiful views for those who traverse it, the Cuillin has mist-shrouded peaks of over three thousand feet. Climbers discovered its worthiness only in the last century, and several of its peaks were named after modern mountaineers. The names, surprisingly, have been Gaelicised, and Sgurr Alasdair — or Alexander's Peak — now commemorates Sheriff Nicolson, the climber who made the first ascent. The Cuillin are also of geological interest as glacial striations and perched boulders are much in evidence.

Skye is rich in history, and aside from fifty to sixty "duns" (or tiny castles) there are the ruins of its four famous castle-fortress and, of course, Dunvegan Castle: the oldest inhabited place of residence in Great Britain and belonging to the Macleod of Macleod. Skye is also the home of two other famous clans, the Macdonalds of Sleat and the Mackinnons who, for hundreds of years, waged war upon one another. Bonnie Prince Charlie, who came "over the sea to Skye", still stalks through the island's memory, for it was here that he came with his loyal followers after losing the Battle of Culloden. Flora Macdonald, who aided the Prince while he was disguised as her Irish maid Betty Burke, is now remembered by a monument at Kilmuir.

Portree is the capital and only town on Skye; however, there are many tiny villages where one can see the scattered population. Skye's economy still rests on crofting, but its great popularity as a tourist resort has much buttressed its finances.

History

Briefly, Skye's history has been characterised by waves of immigration and wars between the clans. Over a thousand years ago the Celts came from Ireland and settled on Skye (legend has it that Cuchullain, the Celtic warrior hero, was among them, but he didn't stay long on the island).

In the ninth century the Vikings arrived, and although they were masters of Skye till the thirteenth century, they made few settlements on the island.

Except for the islanders' participation in the struggles of the Lords of the Isles with the Crown, Skye's history till the eighteenth century was mostly concerned with the wars of the clans : the Macdonalds of Totternish and Sleat, the Mackinnons of the east coast, the Macleods of Lewis (and Vaternish and Dunvegan) and the Macleods of Harris (and Duirinish and Minginish).

On the 19th of August 1745 Prince Charles Edward Stuart landed at Glenfinnan to rally the clans to the Jacobite cause. He was defeated eight months later at Culloden and in April of 1746 he landed on Skye, dressed as Flora Macdonald's maid. The Highlanders did not betray him, even for the Government's reward of £30,000, though many were brought to death or ruin. With Flora's help Prince Charles evaded his pursuers and crossed over the waters to the neighbouring Isle of Raasay, leaving her a lock of his yellow hair.

31

In 1773 Dr. Johnson, accompanied by Boswell, visited the island; in a sense he was the first tourist-explorer to the Western Isles as a whole. While unimpressed by the scenery he was laudatory of the courage of Flora Macdonald, to whom he paid tribute.

During the years 1881 to 1885, after a succession of poor harvests and unsuccessful fishing seasons, Skye was beset by serious riots among the crofters.

The coming of the railway to Kyle of Lochalsh brought people to Skye; the rest we know . . .

How to get there

The only way to reach Skye is by sea, the three departure points being the ports of Glenelg, Kyle of Lochalsh and Mallaig. All three can be reached by car. There are British Rail stations at Kyle of Lochalsh and Mallaig but only bus service to Glenelg.

There are four choices for crossing : there is a car ferry service on the Glenelg-Kylerhea run (address : Glenelg/Kylerhea Car Ferry, Glenelg, Inverness-shire), the Kyle of Lochalsh-Kyleakin run (Caledonian Steam Packet Co.) and the Mallaig-Armadale run (MacBraynes). MacBraynes also run a steamer service from Kyle of Lochalsh and Mallaig to Portree. Only the Caledonian Steam Packet Co. has Sunday runs, but these, as should all other scheduled runs, must be checked before your departure.

Inter- and intra-island travel

If you wish to spend some time on other islands there are a number of services offered to you. MacBraynes run a car ferry service to Tarbert in Harris and Lochmaddy in North Uist; both depart from Uig. Raasay, the tiny island that seems only a step away from Skye, can be reached by a MacBraynes steamer; there is no car ferry service to this island. To reach Benbecula or South Uist, take MacBraynes car ferry from Uig and either drive or take a bus. Barra can be reached by MacBraynes car ferry or steamer from Lochboisdale in South Uist. For Lewis take the MacBraynes car ferry from Uig to Tarbert in Harris; you can drive north or take a bus that passes through Tarbert and goes up as far as Stornoway. For Canna, Rum, Eigg and Muck you will have to return to Mallaig and then go from there to the "Small Isles" on a MacBraynes steamer. To reach the southern islands of Mull, Iona, Coll and Tiree you can either complete the tour of Lochmaddy or Lochboisdale to Castlebay in Barra and from there take a MacBraynes steamer to those islands or return to shore, drive to Oban and take the car ferry to Craignure (on Mull) or the steamer service to the other islands.

The preceding does sound fairly arduous, but MacBraynes have provided for any loss of heart. They do a combined coach and steamer service to South Harris and to Stornoway on Lewis for those who simply want to taste the Outer Hebrides.

A nearby island worth visiting is Raasay which lies just off the mouth of Loch Sligachan and is separated from Skye by the Sound of Raasay. The island is a mere fifteen miles long, with a very uneven coastline. It has a population of only two hundred.

MacBraynes do a combined coach and steamer day-trip to the island which, though slightly regimented, can be quite fun. Inquire about it at the Tourist Office on Skye.

The more adventurous can go by hired launch. Telephone Mr. A. Nicholson at Raasay 226 and he will either pick you up from Sconser Lodge on Skye and transport you to Raasay or vice versa.

For those of you who want to stay on Raasay, accommodation is available at their hotel or their hostel. The former, called Raasay House, is the place where Dr. Johnson and Boswell were entertained by the Macleod of Raasay. It is pleasantly situated on a point overlooking the Sound. The hostel is located further north, near Oskaig. It does not have a store and therefore you must either bring your food from Skye or purchase it from the nearest store at Inverarish, two miles away.

The Nature Conservancy has termed Raasay an "area of special interest" and it is true that it is a favourite beauty spot. There is a profusion of flowers in season and the forests (where there is unrestricted walking) are deliciously inviting. Hilly in parts, the island contains only one mountain, Dun Cann, which is 1,456 feet high. On its flattened top Boswell is reputed to have danced a reel. The ascent is far from difficult. Also of interest is Brochel Castle which is located ten miles north of Raasay House. The castle was once a stronghold of the Macleod's and is now in ruins. At the south end of the island is an iron mine.

From Raasay you can hire a boat to take you to South Rona (to the north) or to Scalpay (to the south). The first is inhabited by the three people who guard the lighthouse; the second possesses the ruins of a chapel which was built on the site of a Culdee cell.

For information about camping on these islands contact the Tourist Office on Skye.

Skye is an island with a particularly good bus service; connections between points can be made with some ease and there is an excellent link-up with the various ports. Schedules can be obtained from the Tourist Office on the island.

Additionally the GPO has introduced a new scheme whereby tourists and residents can be transported to the outlying districts in their mail vans. It is hoped that the service will be continued in 1973.

A number of coach tours (to Elgol and Loch Coruisk, to the Cuillin and Glen Brittle, and to the north end of Skye and Dunvegan Castle) are run by MacBraynes; details about these can be obtained from the Tourist Office on Skye.

Accommodation

Of all the islands, Skye is the best able to provide you with both number and quality in accommodation. There are numerous hotels, guest houses, boarding houses and private houses *all* over the island, not only in Portree. Many of these are situated near places of interest — Dunvegan and Duntuilm Castles, for instance, or Sligachan — and may prove to be more suitable to your needs or your taste than those in "the capital". A variety of sports — fishing, riding, pony trekking, golf, tennis and swimming — are offered at some. Many have such modern amenities as central heating and telephones in bedrooms; some offer reduced rates for children or permit dogs in rooms. A few have facilities for the disabled.

Cottages of all sizes and types, some with and some without the standard amenities, can be rented; their rates usually run from £6.00 to £26.00 a week.

Caravans can be rented from private owners and there are plenty of sites for these and/or for your own throughout the island. Skye also has a number of well-situated camping sites, with many amenities.

Finally, it is the best equipped island for those who frequent youth hostels : there are three on Skye itself and on the nearby island of Raasay.

Detailed information on all of the above can be obtained from the Isle of Skye Tourist Organisation; the price of their Holiday Accommodation Register is 2½p. Or, contact The Scottish Youth Hostels Association, The Camping Club of Great Britain and Ireland Ltd., or the Caravan Club for membership forms and details; their addresses are listed in the Further Information section of The Islands.

As Skye is the most sought after island for holidaying, I *strongly* suggest you book your rooms early, especially for those requiring single rooms.

Eating facilities

Portree, Uig and a number of other villages on the island have good to excellent eating facilities, including tea rooms, cafes and restaurants. In addition, there are many shops which can supply you with the things you need if you are camping or caravanning or staying at a hostel. Hotels, guest houses, boarding houses and the like often serve evening meals.

Sport

Skye excels in some ways over other islands in sporting facilities. There is excellent climbing, fishing and golfing in many areas, in addition to pony trekking, tennis and swimming, though the latter are less prevalent.

Hillwalking and Climbing : We have already mentioned the Cuillin, notable for its beauty, its height and its excellence for climbing. Before I briefly describe a few of its peaks I should like to lend a word of caution : do not attempt to climb to the summits if you are an inexperienced climber. Mist often shrouds the peaks and magnetic compasses often prove to be unreliable here. Both the experienced and the inexperienced should only attempt the Cuillin in calm, clear weather.

Sgurr nan Gillean is the third highest peak on Skye, reaching upwards of 3,167 feet. The best route to take is from the Sligachan Hotel (due west), across the Allt Dearg Mor (Red Burn), near the Cuillin Lodge; follow the sometimes indistinct path that crosses the moorland (due east or left of the peak). Eventually, after a steep climb up the scree, you will reach the south-east ridge of the peak which is a short distance from the top.

Begin the Bruach na Frithe climb in much the same way as the Sgurr nan Gillean, only when you reach the Red Burn cross to Glen Brittle over a pass called the Beallach a' Mhaim. The Bruach na Frithe, which is 3,143 feet, can be reached by climbing the north-west ridge. Care should be taken as the last few hundred feet are narrow.

Sgurr Dearg, the climbing centre of the Cuillin, has many excellent climbs for experienced rock climbers. One way is to climb the west ridge, starting near Glen Brittle House. The Inaccessible Pinnacle is thirty feet higher than Sgurr Dearg's 3,254 feet; the name should give you a clue as to its difficulty.

There are numerous climbs to Sgurr Alasdair which reaches 3,309 feet — the highest peak of the Cuillin. The usual route is the path from Glen Brittle to Coire Lagan and thence up the long, steep scree gully called the Great Stone Shoot. There is some danger here of falling stones. In the centre of the horseshoe ridge is Loch Coruisk, the most superlative of Scottish lochs. The simplest approach to the loch is either by boat from Mallaig or Elgol, or by walking from Strathaird by Camasunary and the side of Loch Scavaig. Watch out for the Bad Step.

The Blaven, which is 3,042 feet, is the highest mountain in the group east of the Cuillin's main range. There should be little difficulty in the ascent from Loch Slapin near the village of Torrin. Follow the stream, Allt na Dunaiche, for about a mile and thence south-west to reach the south-east ridge. The view is magnificent.

The Storr is located on the Totternish peninsula in the north part of Skye. Between Portree and Staffin stands the spectacular pinnacle of the Old Man of Storr, and behind it the Storr itself which rises to 2,360 feet. To climb the Storr go via the steep gully a short distance south of the highest point. The Old Man of Storr and the other pinnacles are difficult and the rocks are treacherously loose. Overlooking the village of Staffin are the Quiraing rocks. To reach these the climber should take the road from Staffin to Uig where the shortest approach is a mile and a half from Staffin. Alternatively a walk north-west below the main line of cliffs brings one to the Needle, while a short, steep climb beyond this point leads to the amphitheatre of cliffs and rock towers called the Prison. The overlooking rocks form a raised platform covered in grass and known as the Table.

Further information can be found in "Scotland for Hillwalking" which is available through The Scottish Tourist Board; the price is 15p. Or, write to The Scottish Youth Hostels Association for details of their mountaineering course at Glen Brittle.

Fishing and Sea Angling : Skye has ideal facilities for fishing in its numerous lochs and bays. Local residents are quite knowledgeable about fishing in their areas and are very willing to help you with any questions. In the event of doubt or difficulty contact the local representative of S.F.S.A.

Before I discuss certain areas let me remind you that a number

37

of hotels have exclusive fishing rights or offer fishing holidays (see Alternative Holidays or contact the Dunvegan Hotel, Dunvegan, Isle of Skye. The proprietors are Jean and Ker Robertson; the latter also happens to be the local representative for S.F.S.A.).

In addition, Captain Henderson in the Glendale area, has a number of boats engaged on wild life courses and has sea angling trips around the isles. Contact Captain N. D. S. Henderson, Hon. Secretary, North West Skye Sea Angling Club, 17 Skindin, Glendale, Isle of Skye.

Further, during 1971 Loch Snizort underwent development and large common skate are now plentiful.

Finally, it is important that you procure the necessary licenses for areas. Information on this, on boat hiring, on where you can get tackle and bait, on the season for fishing and the name of the local representative for S.F.S.A. and his address can be found in the *invaluable* "Scotland for Sea Angling" which is available from The Scottish Tourist Board at a price of 20p. Also a must is "Scotland for Fishing" which costs 25p from the same place.

As we said, Skye offers many possibilities for fishermen and sea anglers. Here are a few of them.

Portree has a good harbour and good fishing facilities; loch, shore and river fishing are plentiful but for the last you will need a permit. Anchorage and berthing are available for visiting craft — there is no charge. The types of fish to be found are cod, haddock, whiting, saithe, lythe and mackerel, in addition to trout and salmon.

Uig has excellent fishing, especially at Loch Snizort and the small islands at its entrance and the Ascrib Islands opposite. You can also fish as far round the coast as Score Bay which is known to some ring net fishermen as the "Golden Mile". The types of fish available are lythe, saithe, mackerel, pollack, conger, whiting, haddock, dogfish, flats, skate, codling and gurnard.

Dunvegan has many noted fishing banks and very deep pools under the sheltered rocky headlands of Loch Dunvegan. Large catches have been landed at Eist Point. Here you will find pollack, halibut, cod, haddock, skate, ling, gurnard, mackerel, dogfish, conger, hake, saithe, whiting and bream.

The seas around the Glendale areas — which are owned by

the crofters of the Glendale Estate and which stretches from Dunvegan Loch, south side, to the Maidens beyond Loch Poolteil and Neist Point — offer tremendous scope for fishing. A sea angling club is also located in this area. You can fish for pollack, saithe and rock cod from the shore and all varieties of sea fish from boats.

Pony Trekking : The Dunvegan Hotel (mentioned previously) caters for a wide variety of sports, including pony trekking. They have a resident instructress and a trek leader who pay special attention to novices. Send S.A.E. for a free brochure.

Shooting : Once again The Dunvegan Hotel caters for this sport which is not as yet that prevalent on Skye.

Golf : Skye has two courses, one at Portree and one at Sconser. Both have nine holes, but only Sconser has clubs for hire. There is no Sunday playing. Further information is available in "Scotland/Home of Golf"; 10p from The Scottish Tourist Board.

Places of interest

We have already alluded to some of the places of interest on Skye; indeed it is an island with so many varied attractions that the visitor will never be at a loss for something to do or to see.

Kyleakin, which is the first place that most visitors set foot in on Skye, is the home of the ruined Castle Maol, a Mackinnon stronghold. It was built in the tenth century by the daughter of a Norwegian king who was the wife of a Macdonald and was usually referred to as "Saucy Mary". It was she who stretched a chain across the Kyle (Kyleakin was derived from the Kyle of Haakon, a Norse king) and tried to levy tolls from passing ships. Offshore is the tiny green island of Pabay, rich in fossils.

Near Broadford and at the foot of the Red Hills is the ruined cottage Coire Chatachan, the house where Dr Johnson and Boswell were guests. This is also Mackinnon territory, and from here you can see the two peaks of Beinn na Caillich and Beinn Dearg Mhor.

On the road north west from Broadford (a well-known tourist centre) there are the Red Hills to one side and the island of Scalpay to the other. The latter, which is separated from Skye by only a narrow sound, has a chapel on the site of a Culdee cell. Eventually the road sweeps around one of the many beautiful sea lochs on Skye, Loch Ainort, the home of the heron and the red deer; Loch Ainort is overlooked by the mountains of Glas Beinn Mhorr and Marsco.

Further north and west are the Red Cuillin and Loch Sligachan, a favourite resort for mountaineers and anglers. In the mouth of the loch, and separated from Skye by the Sound of Raasay, is the island of Raasay. Raasay House, where Johnson and Boswell were entertained by the Macleod of Raasay, is located here, as is Brochel Castle, a ruined stronghold of the Macleods. An excursion can be made to Raasay on a MacBraynes steamer.

Portree, the capital of Skye, was named for King James the Fifth of Scotland who landed there in 1540; Portree is Gaelic for King's Haven. It is, of course, for many, *the* tourist centre of Skye.

In Portree one can see the room where Flora Macdonald took leave of Bonnie Prince Charlie before he made his way to Raasay (go to the Royal Hotel and they will point it out to you). Portree is truly a lovely town, with much charm and grace in its architecture. It has a population of two thousand, which is a quarter of the total population of Skye. It is here the Skye Gathering is held, with much piping and dancing and tossing the caber, and also the cattle shows. Tweeds and tartans are woven in Portree and many shops sell them.

North of Portree is the Storr (see Hillwalking and Climbing) with its obelisk-shaped Old Man. Nearby, on the seashore east of Loch Fada, is the cave where Bonnie Prince Charlie landed from Raasay, spending the night two miles further south. The cave can be approached by a boat. Also at Loch Fada and Loch Feathan is a hydro-electric power station.

From Storr one can go to the Quiraing (see Hillwalking and Climbing) on the Totternish peninsula. Nearby, at Flodigarry, is the home where Flora Macdonald lived during her first years of marriage.

Totternish — the name signifies Thronds's Ness or Cape in Norse — applies to the whole peninsula from Portree in the south to Rudha Hunish in the north. There are still more Flora Macdonald-Bonnie Prince Charlie associations here : at Kilbride the Prince (disguised as Betty Burke) landed from Benbecula with Flora Macdonald, and at Kingsburgh he later found refuge.

After reaching Sgurr Mhor, turn west and south around the shores of Loch Snizort and look towards the other "wing tip" of Skye, Vaternish or "Water Ness" to the Norse invaders. Here one can see many abandoned old crofts, nestling in the hillsides, with their stone dykes which remind the onlooker how the little fields were cleared laboriously by hand. Here one can also see the "black houses" with their beaten earth floors and their fires placed in the centre. At one time part of the black house could be partitioned off to provide shelter for hens and other animals.

Duntuilm Bay, the northernmost point of the roads of Skye, is located in Trotternish. The ruins of Duntuilm, the ancient fortress of the Macdonalds, can be seen here, as can the place where their galleys were drawn up for their ships. Legends abound concerning the departure of the chieftain and his family : the first reason was that the castle was haunted, and the second was that one of the Macdonald babies wriggled from its nurse's hands and was dashed to death on the rocks below. Close by is the old garden, for which the soil was brought from seven foreign kingdoms.

Uig Bay nestles in the arms of Loch Snizort and on its shores is the village of Uig. South of Uig is Kingsburgh House, built on the site of the residence which housed Bonnie Prince Charlie. Dr Johnson occupied the same bed some years later but "had no ambitious thoughts about it". It was here that Dr Johnson met Flora Macdonald who had returned from her exile in America. Flora Macdonald is buried at Kilmuir and on her monument is inscribed Dr Johnson's tribute to her. Nearby is the Skye Cottage Museum.

From Sligachen one can visit Dunvegan Castle and its surrounding places of interest. Now we are in Duirinish where one can see the two chief hills called Macleods Tables; Dunvegan Head, on the northernmost extremity of Duirinish, which are black cliffs one hundred feet high; and, off Idrigill Point, on the southern end, the three basaltic stacks called Macleod's Maidens.

41

Dunvegan Castle is one mile from the village of Dunvegan; once it was accessible only by sea. Now you can reach it via the bridge thrown across the ravine which formerly served as the moat. Dunvegan Castle, the most historic building on Skye, is a hulking mass which shows every style from the fifteenth to the nineteenth century. Since "time immemorial" this has been the seat of the Macleod of Macleod. It has been said that the tower can be dated in the fifteenth century. A dungeon can be entered from the second floor near the drawing-room. In the South tower is the Fairy Room (sixteenth century); a connecting dining room was built a century later.

The main point of interest, of course, is the Fairy Flag which has been preserved in a glass case. Tradition has had it that it would save the clan in three great dangers, but if it was waved for a trivial reason then a curse would fall on the Macleods. The first two times it was waved by Macleods and did in fact help them win a battle and end a cattle plague. The third time it was waved by the Macleod's factor, a man named Buchanan, in 1799; his curiosity resulted in disaster for the family ... Also preserved in the castle is an ancient Irish cup of bog-oak (belonging to Rory More, Sir Roderick Macleod, the twelfth century chief), relics of Bonnie Prince Charlie and letters from Dr. Johnson and Scott in which they refer to their visits.

Not far away from Dunvegan is the legendary Macrimmon school of piping at Bororaig Glendale. Further down the western seaboard are Lochs Bracadale and Harport, and Carbost, the site of the famous Talisker distillery. Minginish, where these places are, is also the site of the Black Cuillin. These are formed of black gabbro, but when the light shines on them they have a blue tint.

Also to be visited are Loch Coruisk and Loch Scavaig at the foot of the Cuillin. Simply take a boat from Elgol, across Loch Scavaig to the land-locked Loch Coruisk. In this area, off the mouth of Loch Scavaig, is the Isle of Soay. Here is the site of an unsuccessful venture whereby oil was extracted and skins were processed of basking sharks. Most of the islands inhabitants were removed to Mull, in 1953, but a few farmers reoccupied it a year later.

Between Armadale and Broadford one can see Dunscaith Castle, another ruined keep of the Macdonalds. Knock Castle, another Macdonald stronghold, was occupied by the family till the seventeenth century. At present they reside in Armadale Castle, built in the early part of the nineteenth century; Dr. Johnson and Boswell were entertained here, but Johnson found it none too pleasing. The point of Sleat, the southernmost area of Skye, is five miles away.

Specialised interests

Skye, though not the most notable island for those with specialised interests, does cater for some. Over seventy different types of birds have been spotted; these range from the sparrow to the golden eagle. A variety of flowers can be seen. The Cuillin, of course, have geological interest. Painters and photographers, though, are probably best rewarded as Skye is, quite simply, beautiful.

Further information

Events include : Skye Week (usually held during the last week of May); the Skye Agricultural Show (usually the last Friday in July); Highland Games and Macrimmon Memorial Silver Chanter Competition (in 1972 they were held on the 19th of August); and British Legion Week (from the 6th to the 10th of September in 1972).

Local information

Isle of Skye Tourist Organisation, Meall House, Portree, Isle of Skye, Inverness-shire.

Canna

Sanday

Kilmory

Kinloch Castle

Rhum

● Harris

Trollaval

Muck

THE SMALL ISLES

Description

To the south of Skye and to the north of Coll, Tiree and Mull lie the Small Isles: Rum (sometimes spelled or misspelled Rhum), Eigg, Canna and Muck.

Though not forgotten, these islands are usually considered to be somewhat off the tourist track except, of course, for those who cruise around them on a MacBraynes steamer from Mallaig. Still, these islands are treasured by many for their geological, botanical and ornithological interests; it is hoped, therefore, that you will have sufficient time (or natural curiosity) to fit them in on your holiday.

Rum is a barren, mountainous island with three peaks over 2,500 feet. It is the largest of this group of islands, measuring eight miles square. Its history dates back to Roman times, with a mention being made of the Blood Stone Hills. The blood stone was in fact mined on Rum for centuries and the last slab was made into a table top for Queen Victoria. In 1826 the entire population, except for one family, was forced to evacuate the island. From 1888 - 1957 it belonged to the estate of the Bulloughs of Lancashire; it then was sold and now it belongs to the Nature Conservancy. At present the total population is around forty, the majority of whom live near Kinloch.

To the south east of Rum lies the smaller island of Eigg (pronounced "egg"). It measures five miles by two and a half miles. The most conspicuous — if not curious — landmark is a basaltic peak which is called the Sgurr of Eigg; it measures 1,289 feet. A similar peak also exists at the north side of the island. In the sixteenth century it was the scene of a terrible tragedy; two hundred Macdonalds were suffocated in a cave near the south east shore when the Macleods of Skye lit a fire at its entrance in an attempt to avenge a supposed wrong. Scott maintains that he "brought off a skull from among the numerous specimens of mortality which the cavern afforded". Presently the small population of the island is employed by Sir Steven Runciman on his estate.

Canna, a fertile island which lies to the north west of Rum, has sometimes been referred to as the "Garden of the Hebrides". It measures a mere four and a half by three-quarter miles. A cliff, which measures only 690 feet above sea level, is the highest point on the island. It is known as Compass Hill as its alleged magnetic effects alter the compass readings on ships. The island has a population of sixty.

Finally, Muck, the smallest of the Small Isles and the most southerly of the group, is a mere two miles long. Its name, in Gaelic, is "Muic" or "sea-pig" and it is often referred to as "Porpoise Island". The island has lovely sandy beaches along the coast and a harbour at Port Mor. The population was once employed on the estate of Laurence MacEwan, until his death in 1939. All that remains are six families.

How to get there

Day-trippers always take the "Small Isles" cruise which is run by a MacBraynes steamer three times a week. Those wishing to land are then transferred (and picked up at a later time) from the ship by ferryboat; at this time one can land on Eigg, Muck and Rum. Two times a week a MacBraynes steamer visits Canna, Rum and Eigg; transfers can only be made to the latter two islands.

Inter- and intra-island travel

For island hopping simply use the aforementioned service. From Canna one can go by Sanday, another island, by crossing a bridge at the end; on Sunday one will find a little modern shrine.

Accommodation

Accommodation might prove to be a problem on the Small Isles; however there are ways... There are no hotels or guest houses on Rum and. in the main, only day visits to Kinloch Castle are permitted. The island, as we said, is a Nature Reserve and is therefore restricted. If you wish to *camp* on the island you must seek the permission of The Nature Conservancy (The Nature Conservancy, 12 Hope Terrace, Edinburgh EH9 2AS).

For caravanning write to Mr. A. J. MacKinnon, Cleadale. Isle of Eigg and ask if you can rent one or the other of his caravans (the cost is £7.00 - £12.00 per week). To camp you must contact The Factor, Eigg Estates Ltd., Isle of Eigg, Inverness-shire for permission.

Canna has a number of bed and breakfast cottages; for information about these write to The Fort William and District Tourist Organisation, Cameron Square, Fort William, Inverness-shire.

Muck, unfortunately, does not have any facilities for overnight visitors.

Eating facilities

For those who wish to stay on one or more islands, I would suggest bringing your own food, except, of course, where food is provided. Shops are few in number and supplies are limited.

Sport

The Small Isles are good for climbing, hillwalking and fishing. Rum has some magnificent peaks, culminating in Askival which is 2,659 feet high. The basaltic peak, Sgurr of Eigg, is well worth a good climb — where possible. The Sgurr itself is columnar, having been poured forth in a molten state. Similarly, the base of the cliff on the north side of the island may also be attempted. On Canna you can climb the fine cliffs in the western part or Compass Hill in the north east.

Places of interest

Rum offers a number of sights for tourists and specialists alike. The most important is Kinloch Castle which was built by one of the Bulloughs in 1901. The architecture will take you back: it is a miniature "classical" mausoleum. Mc-Culluch has described it as a "sawed off baronial pile". It stands two storeys high and has a pillared front. There is a glass-roofed promenade all around its walls and it is surrounded by spacious lawns and gardens. The Blood Stones Hills can be visited as can the ruined village around the little bay of Kilmory. For the intrepid there are the mountains.

On Eigg, the Sgurr of Eigg is much in evidence. The cave where the Macdonalds perished can still be seen on the south east shore. In Kildonnan churchyard there is a marvellous Celtic cross-slab. On the west side, four miles north of Glamidale pier, are the "Singing Sands" or "musical sands" in the bay of Camas Sgiotaig.

Visit Compass Hill on Canna, but be sure to bring along your compass. Near the harbour, on the summit of a lofty stac, are the ruins of a tower; it is reputed that the jealous Lord of the Isles kept his beautiful foreign bride within its walls. Canna Church, which was built in 1914, has a round tower of some note. A quarter of a mile north of the post office is a finely sculptured, though, unfortunately, mutilated cross, in addition to the unexcavated remains of a small Celtic nunnery. Visit Sanday via the bridge — for the walk and for the shrine.

Take a brisk tour of Muck and be sure that you view its beaches and harbour.

Specialised interests

Rum, as we said, is a Nature Reserve and at present its people are carrying on experiments there into the restoration of woodland. Rum is also the main place in Britian for the study of red deer, of which they have over 1,500. The Rum mouse is also in some abundance. Rum also has the largest

Manx shearwater colony in Britain, plus many sea birds, eiders, red-breasted mergansers and other Hebridean birds. (For more information on these, write to P. Wormell, The White House, Kinloch, Isle of Rum).

The mountains of Rum provide much geological interest, mainly for their volcanic origin and for their composition. Also of note for geologists are the Sgurr of Eigg, the "Singing Sands" (Eigg) and Compass Hill (Canna).

Local information

The Fort William and District Tourist Organisation, Cameron Square, Fort William, Inverness-shire.

The Nature Conservancy, 12 Hope Terrace, Edinburgh EH9 2AS.

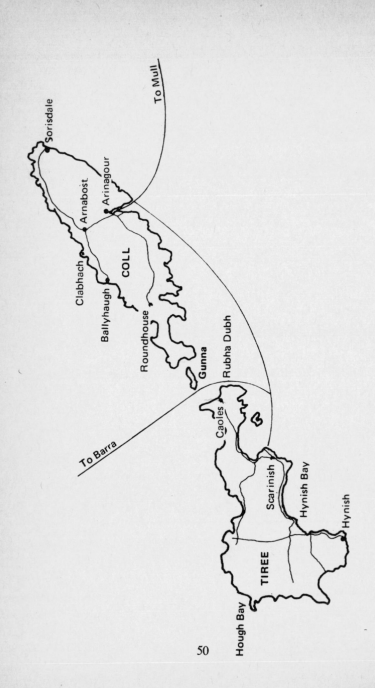

COLL AND TIREE

Description

To the south and south west of the Small Isles are the islands
of Coll and Tiree, the latter two separated from each other
by only a few miles of water, the Sound of Gunna.

Though similar in shape to Tiree, Coll is the smaller of the
two, measuring only twelve miles in length and three miles
in width. The island's treeless surface undulates softly with
rich, arable farm land, and hills that reach no higher than
three hundred and thirty-nine feet. The east coast is rocky
while the west is bound with some beautiful beaches and bays.
In the north are located twenty-eight of Coll's forty trout-
filled lochs, and close to these you can see numerous brochs,
evidence of the island's earlier history. Crofting is the mainstay of Coll's prosperous population, which now numbers
less than one hundred and fifty.

Although hardly large (it is two miles longer and three miles
wider than Coll), Tiree supports a population of almost one
thousand people, the majority being crofters or bulb-growers.
Tiree is the flatter, though similarly fertile, and its scenery
burns brightly in a vast profusion of colours.

Coll and Tiree are a delight for those who like a quiet, rest-
ful holiday ... in the sun. Indeed the islands, Tiree in particular, have been noted for their especially warm and sunny
climate. Investigation has borne this out : in the month of
June in 1971, Tiree had an average of slightly more than two
hundred and fifty-six sunshine hours — the greatest of the
Hebridean islands !

The inducements are many : clear skies and wide horizons,
lovely deserted beaches, calm blue waters for a leisurely
swim, fish — heavy lochs — even a golf course ! And while

there's so much to see — duns, brochs, caves, castles and chapels — you never feel hurried, as the pace of the islands is slow and easy. Even the specialist won't sense any particular need to scramble over cliffs to note down the bird life or crawl around ruins and call out dates. Because there's time, and a great deal of it on Coll and Tiree . . .

History

Sharing the history of the rest of the Hebrides, Coll passed quietly from pre-history into the tumultuous Viking invasions. Later the island fell under the sway of Somerled and the Clan Donald Lords of the Isles. The Donalds then granted the island to the Macleans of Mull who held onto it until 1865. It is said that the Macleans impoverished themselves by buying food for the islanders whose population, at that time, numbered fifteen hundred. Evictions were, in fact, a necessity as the land could not support such a large population. Therefore between the years 1841 and 1861 half of the inhabitants were re-settled in Canada and Australia.

Coll was then broken up into farms and later re-colonized by dairy-farmers from Kintyre and Ayrshire. There was a brief moment of prosperity before the First World War as the farmers were exporting huge quantities of milk and the once famous Coll cheese. The collapse of the industries during and after the war spurred the farmers to breed beef cattle instead, a factor which, according to The West Highland Survey of 1944 - 50, would spell its end. Unfortunately the farmers persisted — rather than returning to dairy farming — and hence there is the steady decline of the island's population.

Tiree's beginnings mirror Coll's — to a point. It too suffered from the Norse invasions and, eventually, it came under the aegis of the Lords of the Isles who granted it to the Macleans of Mull. The Macleans achieved independence in 1476, but over a century later they invaded Islay and their chief died in battle. The island was then given to the Campbells of Argyll; the present duke is still the owner.

The island's population reached almost forty five hundred

people in 1831, over four times what it is today. The Clearances, combined with the ruining of their fishing industry because of poaching, contributed to the decline of the population; it is now fairly stabilised. In the 1950s the island introduced bulb growing, with some success. It is now Tiree's second industry, in addition to stock raising.

How to get there

Both islands are very accessible. MacBraynes run a direct, almost daily service from Oban, stopping first at Coll. The same company also does day trips to the islands from Oban and from Tobermory and Craignure on Mull. Contact MacBraynes for a timetable of sailings.

During the summer Loganair run a daily flight from Glasgow Airport to Reef Airport on Tiree; in winter the service is cut down to four times a week. Flying time is only an hour. Loganair also do weekend flights to Coll.

Inter- and intra-island travel

You can easily travel from Coll to Tiree or the reverse on a MacBraynes steamer. If, however, your timetable doesn't coincide with theirs you can easily hire a boat to take you from one to the other.

To go slightly further afield you can take a MacBraynes steamer directly to Mull from the islands and then proceed to Iona.

The Outer Hebrides can also be reached from Coll and Tiree. There is a not terribly frequent service from the islands to Castlebay on Barra and from there to Lochboisdale in South Uist.

Travel on the islands is mainly on foot, or by car, but Tiree does have a minibus service which also does island tours. Contact Alexander Sinclair, Clachan Guest House, Baugh, Tiree for further information.

Accommodation

Coll has only limited accommodation facilities for the visitor. There is one hotel (the owners have cars and bicycles for hire to both residents and non-residents), one cottage, a few bed and breakfast houses and some camping and caravanning areas on the west coast dunes. To be assured of space book early or take an all inclusive holiday as offered by the Highlands and Islands Development Board.

Tiree is better equipped for tourists. There is a hotel at Scarinish and a number of cottages, guest houses, and bed and breakfast places scattered throughout the island.

For information on both islands' accommodation facilities write to The Oban, Mull and District Tourist Organisation.

Eating facilities

Here, as well as on some of the other islands, there are "food problems". Meals can be obtained at the place where you are staying. These can be supplemented by the food at the local shops (especially on Tiree). If in doubt bring food from the mainland.

Sport

Fishing and Sea Angling : Fishing, especially for brown trout, is perhaps better on Coll, as is sea angling. A permit to fish on the Coll Estate can be obtained from The Factor, Coll Estate House, Arinagour, Isle of Coll. For the angler there are fairly plentiful mackerel, saithe, lythe, codling, conger, haddock, grey mullet, skate, flounder and shark — mainly on the Atlantic side of the island. For additional information write to The Scottish Tourist Board and ask for their pamphlets "Scotland for Sea Angling" and "Scotland for Fishing" (20p and 25p respectively).

Golf : Tiree has a nine hole golf course, located at Vaul.

You will have to bring your own clubs as there are none for hire. Playing is not permitted on Sundays.

Swimming : The beaches of Coll and Tiree are completely unspoiled and the water is brilliantly clear and calm. Some of the best beaches are located at Feall Bay and A Chroic (on Coll) and Scarinish, Traigh Bhi at Balephuill, and Loch Valla (on Tiree).

Wildfowling : Both islands have been noted for wildfowling. I would suggest that you check with the British Field Sports Society, Haig House, 23 Drumsheugh Gardens, Edinburgh 1 for details.

Places of interest

On Coll :

Two Castles on Coll must be visited. The first is called Breachacha Castle, an almost completely-intact fourteenth-century stronghold of the Macleans of Coll. Dr Johnson, it is said, was fascinated by it on his trip to the island in 1773. Nearby is an eighteenth century "mock castle" which was erected by the Macleans when they found their original castle no longer inhabitable. Dr Johnson is reputed to have said that it looked like a "tradesman's box". Both are located on the south west end of the island.

At Arnabost, on the site of a ruined schoolhouse, stands an ancient earth house. The entrance to it is under the school's porch, and from there you can crawl along an underground passage for forty feet. When excavated the earth house was found to contain various implements, brooches, pins and a vase.

At the summit of Coll's highest hill, Ben Hogh (three hundred and thirty nine feet) is a boulder which was left stranded by an Ice Age glacier; it is so delicately balanced on three stones that it can be rocked with ease.

On the road to Totronald are a number of standing stones called Na Sgialachan or "The Tellers of Tales". They are thought to belong to a pre-Druidic period, although their exact origin and purpose are under debate.

On a hillock to the left of Loch Ithiurine is a pagan burial site — the Cnoc a Bhadain — where a number of stone cists are visible.

Coll's cemetery, Cill Ionnaig, is situated in a hollow beyond the Windy Gap. The cemetery is divided into three parts, with the oldest section nearest the stream. Here you can see the remains of a pre-Reformation chapel and some tombstones with the Maclean of Coll arms. Another group of stone cists, dating from the pre-Christian era, are located just over the hill. Also of interest is the Malin Workshop at Crossapol where Mr and Mrs R. Hedderwick produce attractive prints of the Hebrides.

On Tiree :

On the north shore of Balephetrish is the Clach a' Choire (the "Stone of Corrie") — a huge boulder poised on a rocky base with a hollow space between. It is deeply pitted with cup markings which are believed to have once been connected with some ancient form of worship.

Standing on a promotory between Traigh an Duin and Traigh Bhaigh are the ruins of the fort of Dun Heanish, the first of the many forts that can be seen on the island.

Reef Airport is, naturally, on the site of a reef, though this one covers almost a thousand acres. In the area are two raised beaches which distinctly show the sea limits of former days. Here, too, are the ruins of St. Finan's Chapel.

Near the summit of Moidhir-mheall stands a broken off rock called Spitheag an Fhomhair or the Giant's Chip. According to tradition a dweller in one of the Kenavara caves threw the stone (which is approximately eleven feet high and five and a half feet wide) over four miles in retaliation for someone intruding on his sanctuary.

At one time a church was situated at Kilmolvaig, but of this there is no trace. However it is said that ploughmen often find human remains on the site of the graveyard.

On the western slope of Beinn Hough is The Well of the Nine Living. Tradition has it that a widow who resided near this spot kept herself and her family of eight alive on shell fish and the waters of this well.

The remains of the chapel of St. Kenneth are located in the western part of the township of Kilkenneth. Half a mile west are the remnants of numerous cairns, some of them connected by causeways and placed in rows which go from north to south. It is believed that these are from the Viking period. Similar cairns may be seen a quarter of a mile from Dun Hainis.

Different sorts of cairns are located at Baile-Meadhonach : these consist of two concentric circles, the innermost being paved with large, rounded quartz pebbles. Adjoining the ruins is the old Christian burial ground Cnoc a' Chlaidh.

In the area around Kenavara there is much to be seen. On the west side of Kenavara point is Dun na Gall, a Viking fort. On the hill of Kenavara are two caves. The first, An Uamh Mhor, or The Great Cave, has a boulder at its mouth which must be climbed before you can enter the cave. The cave itself is reputed to go so far back that a lighted candle will cease to burn because of a lack of oxygen. The other cave, to the south west, can only be entered by means of a rope. Kenavara should be explored as it is a veritable garden of blue-bells, clover and geraniums, in addition to being a sanctuary for sea birds.

Ten miles off the point of Hynish is the lonely Skerryvore Lighthouse. A feat of engineering in its day (1843), the lighthouse has ceased to have been inhabited in recent years. Its light still flashes over a twenty-one mile radius.

At Soroby are some interesting antiquities : a memorial stone in the form of a massive bossed cross; an ancient trough stone of the type usually associated with Iona (Tiree was once used as "Iona's Granary"); and two eighteenth-century tablestones. The most prized stone is dedicated to Anna, prioress of Iona. On the upper part in bold relief is a representation of St. Michael and the dragon, and near the foot is the figure of death holding a nun by the hand. The inscription, in raised Gothic letters, is located between the two sets of figures.

The oldest relic of antiquity on the island is a standing stone reputed to be from Druid times. This is located at Balinoe.

On Loch an Eilein, on the site of the ancient castle of the Macleans of Tiree, is the Island House, built by the Earl of Argyll in 1748. Between the Island House and the shore is a sandy knoll known as Bac a' Chroichaidh, the Hanging Knoll, where hangings once took place.

At Kirkapol are the remains of three chapels, one of them

eight or nine hundred years old. Here, too are eight sculptured slabs or trough stones.

Two excellent specimens of brochs can be seen at Vaul : the larger is called Dun Mor Valla (Big Fort of Vaul) and the smaller, appropriately, is called Dun Beag Valla (Little Fort of Vaul). The second is situated a quarter of a mile from the first. Both have been dated between the first and the third century A.D.

On an isolated rock at the east end of Salum Bay is An Dunan, another small fort. A massive causeway links it to the shores. Traces of another ancient causeway, leading to a former tidal island, can be seen to the north east.

Finally, at Caolas, is the semi-broch Dun Mor a' Chaolais; its ruins can be viewed from almost every spot on the island.

Specialised interests

There are many finds for the archæologist on these islands. Duns, cairns and brochs are in some abundance and, because many are not marked, it is up to you to find them for yourselves.

The bird life is also of interest. Here you will see the grey lag goose, sheld duck, terns, oystercatchers, gannets, terns, starlings, sparrows and shags, to name a few.

On Tiree, especially, there is a wide variety of flowers growing in vast profusion. The island now considers itself a "Little Holland" because of its bulb growing.

Local information

The Oban, Mull and District Tourist Organisation, Albany Street, Oban, Argyll.

To Coll

Tobermory

Dervaig

Calgary

Ulva

L. na Kael

Salen

MULL

Craignure

Ben More

Lochdonhead

L. Scridain

Lochbuie

Fionnphort

Bunessan

Ross of Mull

Carsaig

MULL AND THE OTHER INNER ISLES

Description

During the last few years, more and more tourists have been choosing Mull as their holiday resort — and who could blame them. Here is an island that offers so much to so many in the way of sights, sports and pure entertainment that even those of you who feel particularly jaded after a long winter will respond to its pleasures.

Mull is mountainous and for this reason it has been appropriately named "a mass of hill". Its scenery, however, is even more wide ranging than this : there are wonderful sandy bays, deep pine forests, a profusion of flowering shrubs and cool, clear lochs. It is alternately stern, wild and charming, but the overall atmosphere is one of serenity.

The third largest of the Hebridean islands, Mull is over thirty miles in length; however it is so indented with sea lochs and creeks that it is only three miles from sea to sea between the Sound of Mull at Salen and the Atlantic at Loch na Keal. The almost three hundred miles of coastline and one hundred miles of roads give the tourist much scope to explore — and to gaze. For Mull is beautiful, and undoubtedly its wide-ranging visual appeal has made it into the "little Hollywood" for film-makers.

The main centre of this island is the town of Tobermory which stands on the shore and slopes of a picturesque, thick-wooded bay, sheltered by the islet of Calve.

Tobermory means "Well of St. Mary" or "St. Mary's Well" and, appropriately, the St. Mary's Well is located to the north west of the town: at one time it was believed to have healing virtues.

In Tobermory Bay lies the sunken wreckage of a Spanish galleon, the "Florencia" or "Florida". Many attempts have been made to retrieve its treasures, and although these have been by and large unsuccessful, they have proved to be a constant source of interest to islanders and tourists alike.

Dr. Johnson visited Tobermory in October of 1873. Unfortunately a storm, a tiring ride from Ulva and the loss of his oak stick put him out of sorts with this charming place.

Some time later, Isabella Bird, the traveller and the first woman fellow of the Royal Geographical Society, occupied a house in Tobermory for several years.

One of the most exciting sights on the island is Ben More, a very accessible mountain of 3,169 feet. Not only is it a mountain of great beauty, but also it is one of the most recently active volcanoes in the west of Europe. Truly the "king of Mull", Ben More offers those who ascend it a most commanding view, spanning from Islay (to the south) and around and up to the Outer Hebrides (to the north and north west). Unlike some of the peaks we encountered on Skye, Ben More can be ascended with ease, even by the inexperienced.

Another attraction on the island is Duart Castle which is located on the headland. This ancient castle was confiscated after Culloden. It was repurchased and restored in 1912, and now, after one hundred and fifty years of alienation, it is again the seat of the chief of the Macleans. It is open to the public throughout the summer months.

The region around Loch na Keal abounds in prehistoric monuments, including the standing stones at Dervaig and a galleried fort (dated around the first century, B.C.) at Burg.

For many years the island of Mull was under the shadow of Iona and only now, in the twentieth century, has Mull begun to come into its own. The offerings, to be sure, are different. Mull was the scene of wars between clans, whereas Iona was the centre of religious activities. Mull, in a sense, has more for the general tourist, for the sportsman and for those with specialised interests; Iona remains a "Sacred Isle" with many of its religious monuments lovingly restored. Mull does not begrude this, and one will see, in the south of the island, sign after sign, road after road, leading to Iona. And you can go there easily, as MacBraynes run a steamer from Mull.

Mull is a many-faceted island, and one which caters to the arts. It sports a school of painting and, in the north west of the island at Dervaig, one of Scotland's smallest theatres, the Mull Little Theatre. The theatre is run by two people, and plays are performed regularly throughout the summer.

Sporting facilities are in abundance. These include golf (there is a nine hole golf course), tennis, shooting, pony trekking, climbing and sailing.

Finally, Mull is an island which stages many events, and not the least of these is Mull Week, which takes place at the beginning of May each year. Ceilidhs are held in Tobermory, Dervaig, Salen, Craignure and Bunessan, with well known Scottish artistes joining the local performers. In addition, there are dances, barbeques, plays, treasure hunts and many outdoor events.

The Mull Highland Games, held at Tobermory on the first Thursday of the Glasgow Fair, are reputed to be one of the most famous in Scotland. The games field, a natural amphitheatre high on a hill behind Tobermory, affords spectators a superb view of the events.

In October, Mull is the scene of a Motor Car Rally. The car rally, the first that was ever staged in the Hebrides, has been running since 1969.

History

Mull has a checquered past. Like so many of the islands in the Hebrides, Mull was the scene of Celtic settlement and clan warfare. The Macleans were once vassals of the Lord of the Isles, but the clan became independent in 1476. At one point in history the Maclaines of Lochbuie disputed the chiefship of Clan Gillean with the Macleans of Duart, but the Crown upheld Duart as the chief of the clan and "Laird of Maclean". Duart Castle was lost after the '45 and the island was later subjected to the Clearances. In 1953 the Soay islanders were re-settled on Mull, though many later left for the mainland.

How to get there

Mull is fortunate in that it has three ports: Tobermory, Salen and Craignure. Additionally, not only one port but

three service the island : Oban, Lochaline and Mingary. Mac-
Braynes, of course, do all of the sailings. Only one is a car
ferry service : Oban to Craignure. MacBraynes also run a
regular launch service from Kilchoan (Ardnamurchan) on the
mainland which goes to Tobermory. There is a good connecting bus service, and passengers who disembark at Craignure can take a bus to Tobermory via Salen. Write to
David MacBrayne for a timetable.

Loganair have a regular summer service between Glasgow,
Oban and Mull (the airstrip is at Glenforsa, near Salen).
For further details write to Loganair Ltd.

Inter- and intra-island travel

MacBraynes, solely and in combination with the bus company, do a series of inter-island tours and voyages which I
strongly recommend to you.

The favourite of these, of course, is the tour to Iona, Staffa
and the Treshnish Isles. Iona, as we said, is the "Sacred
Isle" and it was here that St. Columba founded his monastery in 563. The thirteenth-century Cathedral which succeed-
ed Columba's monastery, the ruined buildings, the Celtic
crosses and the graves of many Scottish kings — to name a
few sights — should be seen.

Staffa, an uninhabited island lying north of Iona, is best
known for its remarkable basaltic caves, the most important of these being Fingal's Cave. It was this cave that
inspired Mendelssohn to write his "Hebrides Overture". Excursion steamers pass close to the caves.

Special tours are run from Tobermory with a stop on Iona
to let you explore its wonders. However if you wish to go to
Staffa, which is a privately owned island, you can take the
Ulva Ferry (from the port of the same name).

Additionally, the Ulva Ferry will also take you to the Treshnish Isles, specifically Lunga. This is the main island of the
group, with a large number of sea birds which nest on its
famous Harp Rock. These islands were once fortified and the
ruins of many strongholds can still be seen, the latest dating

back to 1380. The island is presently uninhabited, the last family having left for the mainland in 1824.

Additional information on these tours and voyages can be obtained from David MacBrayne Ltd., The Oban, Mull and District Tourist Organisation, or the Tourist Office at Tobermory. Further details about the islands will be presented in the following chapter.

There are other choices open to you with respect to inter-island travel. Two islands lie to the west of Mull, surrounded by Loch na Keal and Loch Tuath. These are Ulva and the tiny island of Gometra. The first is well-known for its basaltic columns and the second has lofty cliffs, also of basalt.

Ulva once supported a large population of crofters, six hundred, in fact, during the fifteenth century when it was owned and dominated by the Macquarries. Now only half a dozen families live on the island and all are employed by Lady Congleton who owns it. She it reputed to be a very generous woman : she has provided cottages for the families and the free use of a boat.

General Lachlan Macquarie was born on the island; later he became the governor of New South Wales. Ulva House, where the Macquarie entertained Dr. Johnson and Boswell (preceding their tiring trip to Mull), was burned down in 1954. The small church is in disrepair but is interesting to see. Also to be viewed is the burial ground of the Clark family who once owned the island; it is a curious sight and one writer has described it as resembling "a misplaced sheep-tank".

From Ulva you can go to Gometra — on foot. No cars are allowed on Ulva. The walk is twenty miles, ten each way, from shore to shore. There is a bridge which links them.

The island is also privately owned and is only inhabited by two people. There are, however, over three hundred Blackface sheep and thirty cross Highland cattle grazing there. The land is fertile and each year it produces a good crop of barley, corn, turnips and kale. Be sure to climb the cliffs: there are excellent views of Little Colonsay and Staffa (in the south) and the Treshnish Isles (to the west).

If, by chance, you wish to go to these islands I would suggest that you hire a boat at Ulva Ferry. A number of people have found that staying on privately owned islands is a distinct possibility and these, I believe, are not excepted. Either write to The Oban, Mull and District Tourist Organisation or contact the owners directly for permission.

There are still other possibilities for touring islands in the vicinity. We have already mentioned that Coll and Tiree are reached by MacBraynes and Loganair. However, if you don't mind returning from Mull to Oban, you can visit (by ferry or car) the small islands of Lismore, Kerrera, Seil and Luing, to name only a few.

Lismore is a flat, green and treeless island which lies in outer Loch Linnhe. Until 1507 it was the seat of the Argyll diocese. The humble parish church (built in 1749) incorporated the choir of the tiny cathedral; some mediaeval elements still survive. Further excavation in 1952 revealed the walls of the nave and the west tower. The cathedral has now been completely modernised and is used as a parish church. The pastoral staff of St. Moluag, the Bachull Morr, which has been dated 592, is now, again, on Lismore. On the west coast there are ruins of the episcopal castle of Achanduin and at the south end of the island there is a lighthouse. On view is the "Book of the Dean of Lismore", a sixteenth-century manuscript collection of Gaelic and English poems of interest to those investigating the Ossianic problem. There is a twice-daily service to Lismore from Oban (except on Sundays).

Kerrera, which lies just off Oban, is now a farming community, although once it was the scene of historical events. In 1249 King Alexander III died of a fever on the island after having fought the Lords of Lorne. A hut was prepared for him in a field on Horseshoe Bay which is still known as Dalry (the King's Field); there you can also see the spring from which Alexander drank (the King's Well). In 1263 Haakon of Norway collected his fleet in the Sound of Kerrera before the Battle of Largs. On the south end of the island one can see the ruins of Gylen Castle, once a Macdougall stronghold. Kerrera is reached by a passenger ferry from Oban.

Slate quarrying, until recently, was the mainstay of Seil and Luing, though now both islands are largely devoted to farming. To reach Seil you can either drive or take a bus (there are tours, in addition) as there is a bridge at Clachan which crosses over the Seil Sound. Its name is the "Atlantic Bridge": it was built from plans produced by Telford and completed in 1792. Easdale, a beautiful slate village which nestles under the cliffs of Seil Sound, must be seen for it gives an excellent view of Mull and the Atlantic. A daily ferry from Seil services the islet of Easdale. If you wish to stay on Seil there are two hotels and other tourist accommodation.

Slates from Luing were once used to re-roof Iona Cathedral, but only one man still works at the craft of slate cutting. In recent years Luing cattle — half Highland and half Shorthorn — have been bred on the island. The Cuan ferry at the south end of Seil will take you to Luing free of charge.

For more information on these and other islands off Oban, contact The Oban, Mull and District Tourist Organisation.

Let us now return to Mull. There is a bus service between Craignure, Salen and Tobermory and to other spots on the island. The island also has taxis and cars for hire in these towns and at Aros and Fionnphort.

Accommodation

For accommodation, Mull is one of the best provided for islands. Apart from packages, the island boasts a wide variety of hotels, guest houses, cottages and bed and breakfast places at Bunessan, Craignure, Dervaig, Fionnphort, Pennyghael, Salen, Calgary and more. In a number of places there are caravans for hire, ranging from £1.00 to £3.00 nightly charge; these can also be rented by the week at a much lower rate. Most are fully equipped; some are royal. There is a youth hostel at Tobermory.

An accommodation list can be obtained from The Oban, Mull and District Tourist Organisation.

Eating facilities

Mull is not a "food problem" island in any sense of the word. In addition to the meals provided at the place where you stay, there are a number of restaurants, grills and tea rooms to choose from. The majority of these are located in the aforementioned towns and villages. Both stationary and travelling shops are in abundance and are particularly good for those who camp or have caravans. The hostel has a small store.

Sport

Mull gives you ample scope for indulging in a wide variety of sports.

Hillwalking and Climbing : We mentioned that Ben More presents no great challenge to the climber and the same is true for the majority of mountainous spots on Mull. Hill-walking, rather than climbing, or at least serious climbing, would be more in order.

Fishing and Sea Angling : There is excellent fishing in Mull, especially at the fishing centre of Tobermory. On the west coast one can fish from such points as Calgary Bay, Loch Tuadh, Ballygowan Bay, Ard Fada in Loch Scridain, and Loch Buie. Sea Angling is excellent all the way down the west and south coasts. Here you will be able to catch mackerel, skate, haddock, conger, flatfish, turbot, gurnard and dog-fish. Additional information about places and permits is available in the two books I mentioned previously : "Scotland for Sea Angling" and "Scotland for Fishing" (both from The Scottish Tourist Board, prices 20p and 25p respectively).

Golf : Tobermory boasts a nine hole golf course. Rates are low and clubs are available for hire. In August there is a competition for the MacBrayne Cup; this, and all other competitions, are open to visitors. Sunday playing is permitted. Residents of the Western Isles Hotel at Tobermory can golf free of charge.

Pony Trekking: Knock is the centre for pony trekking. Half-day and full-day tours are available and there are ponies for small children. For more information ask the Tobermory Tourist Office or enquire at Knock Farm (Knock Farm, Gru-line, Mull; telephone Aros 53).

Yachting : Yachting is plentiful on Mull, with anchorage at Bunessan, the Sound of Mull (Salen) and Tobermory (the regatta town). There are a number of regatta events. The main one is in August, following the dates of the Crinan to Oban race and the Oban to Tobermory race. The Clyde Cruising Club Race — the major event in Scottish yachting circles — finishes at Tobermory on the first Monday after the Glasgow Fair. Visitors are welcome to enter the regatta events staged by the Western Isles Yacht Club in Tobermory; the club also runs dinghy races.

Swimming : The best places to swim on Mull are located at Calgary, Croig, Uisken and Fidden. It is also possible to swim at Tobermory (there is a small beach of Calgary sand) and to dive along the pier path towards the lighthouse. A freshwater pool is being built by a farm owner at Arle; it will be open to visitors. The new Glenforsa Hotel near Salen will also have an open air pool.

Places of interest

There are a number of places to see in Mull and many shores to sit by, gazing at lochs dotted with small islands. Let me mention a few.

At Tobermory it might be of some interest to go to the Old Free Church on Main Street where there is a small "local factory" for handweaving tweeds. Visitors are welcome to walk around the workrooms and the display centre; they can also buy tweeds and other products made on the island.

Tobermory Bay, with its sunken Spanish galleon, should not be missed.

There are two favourite walks from Tobermory; the first is to Forest Park and the other is to Bloody Bay. To reach Forest Park you walk along the Aros path or drive along the Tobermory/Salen Road. Forest Park is a "drive-in" forest which is run by The Forestry Commission. A car park is provided.

To reach Bloody Bay take the path along the shores of

Tobermory Bay from a point just behind the pier at the foot of the cliff. In 1439 Bloody Bay was the scene of a great sea battle, with the Macleans of Duart supporting John, Fourth Lord of the Isles, against his rebel son Angus.

For excellent views of Calve Island, the hills on the mainland of Kilchoan and the entrance to Loch Sunart, walk on the wooded path that goes further along the Sound of Mull.

Outside of Dervaig (in the village see the pencil-shaped church tower) on the Dervaig/Tobermory road are two old burial grounds, one of them with standing stones. The region has other relics of antiquity : there is a first-century galleried fort at Burg, which is west of Torloisk, and a ruined broch at Ballygowan Bay between Torloisk and Ulva Ferry.

Legend has it that the people who settled in Canada and founded Calgary were originally from Calgary on Mull. If you drive towards Torloisk you will pass by the beautiful Calgary Bay.

On the south shore of Loch na Keal you can look across at the island of Erosa and the small green islet of Inch Kenneth; Dr. Johnson and Boswell were entertained on the latter by Sir Alan Maclean. Here you can see Inch Kenneth Chapel. Its burial ground has a number of mediaeval monuments, including a figure of a mailed warrior. Apply to Mr. M. MacGillvray at Gribun, then hire a motor-boat to get there.

Ben More, we have said, can be ascended with ease and it is well worth the attempt. In 1851 the Duke of Argyll discovered fossil beds at Ardtun, in the Ross of Mull, which showed that exotic vegetation once grew in the district. It is suggested that you make your descent of this mountain on its south side so that you can see the beautiful Loch Scridain.

North west of Salen, up on a hill at the mouth of Aros, are the ruins of Aros Castle. This was once the seat of the Lords of the Isles and it is said that it is even more ancient than Duart Castle. It was here, in 1608, that the Clan Chiefs submitted to King James (the Sixth of Scotland and the First of England) through Lord Ochiltree.

At Pennyghael there is a ruined chapel of some interest, in addition to two rather fanciful Celtic crosses. These mark the tombs of a chief of the Duart Macleans and his wife. Legend has it that this couple were suspected of necromancy, and hence they were denied burial on sacred ground.

Going west about a mile from Carsaig Bay you can see the Nuns' Cave. Nuns from Iona took shelter there after being driven off the island by over-zealous Reformers. There are a number of curious carvings on the walls.

Three miles west of the Nuns' Cave are the Carsaig Arches. These were cut by the action of the sea through the columnar basalts of an ancient raised beach; they can only be reached at low tide.

Near Rubha na h Uamha, on the extreme westerly tip of the Ardmeanach promontory, is one of the most celebrated fossil trees in the world. It stands forty feet tall and is five feet in diameter. All but the lower three feet of the central core is eroded, and these are presently preserved in cement. It is said that this tree stood in a forest which was swept by the molten lava of a Mull volcano. The surrounding trees either exploded or shrivelled up in the intense heat; only McCulloch's tree, as it is called after its discoverer, withstood it. The tree can only be reached at low tide.

Also of note is the cleft in a burn on the Salen/Gribun road, about four hundred yards to the Gribun side of the milestone denoting six miles to Salen. Here the Macleans sharpened their swords before going into battle; the stone, itself, was supposed to bring them good fortune. The original Leachd a Li is thought to be quite close by to the existing stone.

The oldest road on Mull begins at Grasspoint and leads inland towards Lochdonhead. It was the first part of this road that the pilgrims of early days used on their way to Iona. Later it became the end of a road which drovers traversed when they brought their cattle onto Mull. On your way stop by Loch Buie, a very beautiful loch.

Finally there is Duart Castle, which we have already mentioned and which you surely must see. Here you will view the cell where the Officers of Tobermory's Spanish galleon were confined; many objects of interest in the searoom and banqueting hall; and relics of the Macleans of Duart. In addition there is a unique exhibit of scouting throughout the Commonwealth; the present Lord Maclean, like his father before him, was Chief Scout.

One further note : Mull abounds in monuments — to the great and to the small. The Tourist Office at Tobermory can tell you about these.

Specialised interests

Mull has much for the geologists who study it so exhaustively. On the westerly seaboard one can view rocks of successive periods, some of them 2,600 years old. Columnar basalt, like those on Staffa, are much in evidence. Fossil remains also abound, such as McCulloch's Tree and the Ardtun Leaf Beds at Bunessan (see Places of Interest). On the north shore of Loch Scridain there are sapphires to be found; unfortunately they are not terribly valuable.

The moist climate on Mull has fostered much vegetation There are well over ninety plants which are deemed uncommon, and even some of these are quite rare in the British Isles.

Ornithologists are frequent visitors to Mull as it is an island rich in bird life. Here you will see herons, buzzards, kittiwakes, starlings, eider ducks, merlins, harriers — to mention just a few.

Mull also caters to those who are interested in fish and other forms of animal life.

There is a painting school at Pennyghael. Write to Julia Wroughton, Pennyghael, Isle of Mull, for more information.

Further information

Events on Mull : Mull Theatre and Music Festival (3rd to 7th July in 1972); Mull Highland Games (22nd July); West Highland Yachting Week (3rd to 7th August); Agricultural Show at Salen (19th August); Mull and Iona Week (12th to 18th September); and Mull Car Rally (16th to 17th October).

Local information

The Oban, Mull and District Tourist Organisation, Albany Street, Oban, Argyll.
The Tourist Office, Tobermory, Isle of Mull, Argyll.

Treshnish Isles

Gometra

Ulva

Dutchmans Cap

Little Colonsay

Staffa

Iona

Ross of Mull

IONA, STAFFA
AND THE TRESHNISH ISLES

Description

In the last chapter we examined, quite briefly, Iona, Staffa and the Treshnish Isles, including them in our list of possible day trips from Mull or from Oban. To be sure, if you only have a day or two to spare then I would suggest visiting these islands rather than some of the others you can reach from Oban. However, if you can manage a few more days than this your time will very likely be re-paid with wonder and peace.

For Iona, as many know, is a very special place: a focal point, for centuries, in the Christian world. As Fiona Macleod has written, "To tell the story of Iona is to go back to God and to end in God". It was, and still is, a place of worship, a "Sacred Isle".

In Gaelic or Pictish the island was called Ioua, a name which was used by St. Adamnan some centuries later. It was known, in Irish, as Hy or Y and in modern Gaelic as I (pronounced as "E" in English). In Gaelic it was also known as Innish nam Druidbneach or "Island of the Druids". After the coming of Columba Iona was spoken of as I Chaluim Chille or "Island of Columba of the Church (or Cell)". The exact derivation still rests on supposition: I shona (pronounced ee hona) means the blessed or sacred isle. Additionally, the Hebrew word for Dove is "Iona" and the Latin is "Columba". Whatever is finally decided, it is still important to see that the island itself was a centre of Druid worship long before the birth of Christ and the coming of Columba; it has, indeed, a long history.

Iona is a small island, only three and a half miles long and one and a half miles wide. Everywhere you turn there is some reminder of religion, some association with its past, some evidence of continuing devotion. When people say there is so much to see they mean a seeing with a difference : for Iona's sights must be looked at with an inner eye . . .

As one of the most southerly of the Western Isles it is blessed with a mild climate and very fertile soil; the members of the Iona Community cultivate it now for their own sustenance. Like so many of the Western Isles it is beautiful, but even here it is a beauty that departs even further from the stream of things. There is something pristine about the island, and its scenery is bright and luminous, especially during the spring and summer months, the best times to visit. Or to stay, Iona has long housed men of religion, and it now provides both hotels and guest houses for the many tourists who come there each year.

Staffa, as we noted, is an uninhabited island, famous for its caves (notably Fingal's Cave) and its basaltic formations. It is a tiny, almost oval, island — just one and a half miles in length and width. Its name is derived from the Norse word Staphi-ey which means "the island of staves or pillars". Of these it has many remarkable ones, curious and wonderful to the spectator.

North of Calgary (see Mull) are the Treshnish Isles. The most southerly of these is known as The Dutchman's Cap because of its shape. The largest, to the north, is called Lunga.

History

Iona, as we have already noted, has had a long history. Some sources prefer to allude to its "creation" but we shall begin with a point further on in history.

In the Iron Age, during the first century A.D., the inhabitants of Iona were of Celtic-speaking origin and had connections with those people living on the Atlantic coast of Scotland and Britain. During the pre-Christian period there was a settlement on the west coast of the island. Excavations since 1957 have revealed a little fort (Dun Bhuirg), remains of huts and bits of pottery. It has been supposed that the settlement lasted only a short time and was certainly gone by the time St. Columba came to the island in 563.

Hotly debated is the connection between the Irish Druids, St. Columba and his disciple, Oran. According to legend Oran offered himself up as a sacrifice which was demanded for the new sanctuary according to tradition. Oran was, in fact, the first to die on Iona; however, St. Adamnan, in his life of St. Columba, never mentions him or his death. This is understandable if you only wish to consider St. Columba's Christian, rather than pre-Christian, origins. It is safe to say that if you take into account St. Columba's heritage, which was that of a pagan Celt, then the sacrifice was a possibility.

In any case, St. Columba did land on Iona in 563, along with twelve companions. He made a preliminary stop on Islay but then continued on, coming to rest at Iona because from there he could not see his native shores of Ireland.

On Iona St. Columba founded a monastery, of which nothing remains. To the west of the cloisters, on a hillock known as Tor Abb, one can see the archæological evidence of St. Columba's cell. There is, in addition, the remains of four carved stone crosses and evidence for several wooden ones (the majority are preserved in the museum).

After establishing the monastery, St. Columba set out on his journeys. These resulted in the conversion of the Northern Picts and the consequent extension of Christianity all over Scotland (including the Orkney and Shetland islands) and Iceland as well. St. Columba died on Iona in 597, a short time after St. Augustine landed in Kent to convert the English. Originally St. Columba was buried on Iona but two centuries later his remains were taken to Ireland, but no subsequent traces now exist.

After St. Columba's death Iona became a place for pilgrimages. Scottish kings were buried there until the eleventh century, when it was superseded by Dunfermline. Until the Middle Ages it was also the graveyard of the important West Highland chiefs. In the Reilig Oran, the burial place near to where the Cathedral now stands, lays buried forty-eight Scottish kings, including Kenneth Macalpine, the first king of a united Scotland; Duncan, the so-called victim of Macbeth; and Macbeth himself. Also interred are seven kings of Norway and four kings of Ireland.

During the ninth and tenth centuries Iona was pillaged by Norwegian and Danish pirates, and in 803 they burnt and destroyed the monastery and everything else as well. As life was becoming a bit too precarious, the monks who were spared moved to Kells, taking with them the relics of St. Columba. From that time Kells took over the supremacy of the Columban congregation.

In the years intervening between 1156 and 1203 Reginald, son of Somerled, Lord of the Isles, founded a monastery on Iona for the Benedictines and, a few years later, a nunnery, which eventually became Augustinian. The Benedictines' enclosure only partly covers that of its Celtic predecessor.

From 1507 until the dissolution after 1570, the church served as the cathedral of the See of Argyll. In 1617 it was annexed to the Protestant bishopric of the isles. Loyalty to the Stewart kings was sworn there by the island chieftains, according to the Statutes of Icolmkill in 1607.

Dr Johnson, of course, visited Iona; afterwards he uttered some considerately pious words. Scott found it "desolate and miserable" and Wordsworth wrote three sonnets on it.

In 1899 the cathedral was presented to the Church of Scotland by the Eighth Duke of Argyll, and soon after restoration began. In 1938 Dr George Macleod founded the Iona Community, a religious brotherhood for the training of students. It was their members who thereafter took up the work of excavation and restoration.

Staffa's history is a geological one. At one point in time, believed to be somewhere between twelve and thirty million years ago, Staffa was prey to volcanic eruptions, such as those common to Mull (see Mull, The Fossil Tree), Islay, Rathlin, the Giant's Causeway and the Treshnish Isles. The land was previously covered with lush vegetation and the slow volcanic activity of the basalt lava allowed the trees to grow to full maturity. The straight columns were formed by slow cooling, and the wavy columns were formed by rapid cooling and secondary disturbances. It has been supposed that the caves were shaped some fifteen thousand years after the Ice Age.

Staffa belonged to the Macquarries of Ulva for nine hundred years. In the latter part of the eighteenth century it changed hands four times. It was then sold to a Mr Forman whose family kept it for more than a century. The island is still privately owned.

There were residents on Staffa until 1800. They left because a noise like a cannon shook the island each time there was a westerly gale; this was due to a large stone being moved in a pothole in the Big Gun Cave (Gunna Mor).

The island was virtually unknown until 1772 when scientists, led by Captain Cook's botanist, Sir Joseph Banks, landed there. Banks had heard of this remarkable island from Mr Leach, an Irish visitor, who had visited the island a few days previously. Pennant's "Tour of Scotland" (1774) has the first account of the island.

Thereafter Staffa was visited or written about by such notables as Scott, Keats, Wordsworth, Tennyson and Jules Verne. Fingal's Cave served as an inspiration to Mendelssohn in his overture "The Hebrides".

The Treshnish Isles have a similar geological history. On the islands you will find a ruined fort, built in 1715; the remains of a castle; and a ruined village. The castle was beseiged in James the Fourth's campaign against the Lord of the Isles, and later the Macleans defended it against Cromwell.

How to get there

Iona can be reached from Fort William (a bus plus steamer tour); from Fort William via Oban; and from Oban (either via Tobermory on Mull or directly, almost every day of the week). Ordinarily the steamer passes quite close to Staffa's caves to permit passengers to see them clearly. The day trips are quite long, lasting from nine in the morning to six in the evening if you're departing from Oban; unfortunately the time allowed on Iona is around one hour. (To make the most of your time, be sure that you get on the first boat that takes you from the ship to Iona's pier). All tours and voyages are run by MacBraynes; write to them for their timetable.

For a cruise around Staffa and the Treshnish Isles you can

take the Ulva Ferry (from Ulva Ferry) on Mull. Landing on-shore is not permitted. However, you can hire a boat for the day from the same people (write to C. P. Anderson, Ulva Ferry, Isle of Mull or telephone Ulva Ferry 210) but be sure to book ahead.

Inter- and intra-island travel

To reach Iona, Staffa and the Treshnish Isles you will have to depart from Mull (see above and the chapter on Mull).
You cannot take your car to Iona. This island is small and you can easily walk around the bulk of it in a full day.
With respect to Staffa and the Treshnish Isles you will almost literally hop on and hop off.

Accommodation

Each year over two hundred clergy visit Iona, not to mention the hundreds of young people who come for camping conferences. Iona does have a number of hotels, guest houses, cottages and camp sites, but I must stress that you book early to avoid disappointment.
I have not discovered the owner of Staffa and thus I am not certain if you can camp on the island. If you do intend to do so I would *strongly* advise you to make enquiries and get permission.
The same advice applies to the Treshnish Isles, only here the owner is known: Lady Jean Rankin. I have heard that she permits a few campers to stay on the islands. She suggests Lunga, mainly because there is less difficulty obtaining fresh water. Do ask her about alternative routes to the islands; she is quite helpful.

Eating facilities

On Iona, you can eat at your hotel or guest house.
If you camp or stay in a cottage, bring your own food either
from Oban or Mull; MacBraynes will take the crates ashore.
Needless to say there are no eating facilities on Staffa or on
the Treshnish Isles. If permission to camp is granted, bring
with you sufficient food and water for your stay.
For further information contact The Oban, Mull and District
Tourist Association, Albany Street, Oban, Argyll.

Places of interest

Iona, Staffa and the Treshnish Isles provide a fascinating array
of sights which you can enjoy, contemplate or study. For this
reason I would suggest that you try to allocate two days for
Iona and one or more for the other islands in this group.
The bookstore, located at the side of Iona's cathedral, has a
number of excellent guides and maps for sale.
A little way from the pier, just off the road leading to the
Cathedral, are the ruins of the Nunnery Church which, as
we said, was built in the early part of the thirteenth century;
there are a number of additions, made at the end of that
century. Here you will see part of the nave, with an aisle, and
the adjoining Lady Chapel which retains some of its vaulting.
South of the Nunnery Church are the remains of the cloister
court, the chapter house and the refrectory.
Nearby is the fourteenth century Church of St. Ronan; it
is presently used as a lapidary museum and will be opened on
request. Notice, particularly, among the tombs of the nuns
and priests, the one belonging to the last prioress who died
in 1543. He effigy in hood and cloak occupies half of the slab,
the remainder having broken away.
On the lane is the fifteenth-century Maclean's Cross which is

said to commemorate a Maclean of Duart. The eleven-foot-high crucifix displays a Crucifixion and a beautifully carved leaf-like design.

Almost directly across the way is St. Oran's Cemetery, the Reilig Oran, the oldest Christian burial place in Scotland (see History). In addition to the kings who are buried there are the graves of island chieftains, the ashes of Marjory Kennedy-Fraser, who collected and transcribed Gaelic songs, and Dr. John Beaton of Mull, the physician to James the Sixth.

Adjoining is St. Oran's Chapel, now completely restored; the architecture is Romanesque. Here are the tombs of Lachlan Mackinnon and the first two Lords of the Isles.

After leaving what Johnson termed "this awful ground" proceed to the Cathedral. Here, off to the left, are three crucifixes : St. Martin's Cross (tenth century) which is carved with Runic ornaments and figures; St. John's Cross (tenth century) and the remains of St. Matthew's Cross. To the north west of the nave is St. Columba's shrine, now completely restored. In front of the Cathedral is a preserved section of the Street of the Dead, a roadway of red marble, dated at the thirteenth century.

The Cathedral dates from the sixteenth century but there have been many later additions and restorations. It is cruciform in plan, with a low square tower that has four windows with much elegant tracery. When you are inside notice the arches which support the tower and the carved capitals of the columns. Examine the three Gothic sedilias; the elaborate Sacristy doorway; the Romanesque arches. The Cloister contains two mediaeval pillars; within its grassy centre is the sculpture "The Descent of the Spirit" by Jacques Lipchitz (1960). Be sure to walk completely around the piece and see what you think of it ... There is a guide who will take you around the Cathedral and point out, among other things, the tombs of the Abbots and Dukes.

Within the compass of the Cathedral are a number of other restored monastic buildings : the Chapter House (with a Norman doorway and a double arch supporting the vault); the Refrectory; the Undercroft; the Redorter and the Caretaker's House.

We mentioned that the Cathedral was built only partly on

the original Celtic foundations. On the Celtic side is the small Michael Chapel and the Infirmary, which now serves as a Museum. Inside is Columba's Pillow, which is believed to be his gravestone; the tombstone of Angus Og; the broken Mackinnon's Cross and a number of other tombs of chieftains and priors.

There are many other interesting sights on the island. At Port na Churaich, within Columba's Bay, you will see many mounds and hillocks which are believed to be evidence of former dwellings or the burial places of islanders who settled there originally.

On the beach itself there are sometimes found a number of transparent green stones which are believed to preserve the possessor from drowning. St. Columba sanctified these amulets and curing stones with the Christian symbol of the Cross.

On the west shore is the Spouting Cave. At certain tides and winds tons of sea water are forced through the opening in its roof, producing a loud roaring noise.

The machair (or sandy plain) was the scene, up until one hundred and fifty years ago, of the old pagan ritual of casting into the sea "The Great Porridge"; if the god was propitiated he would, in return, provide seaweed to fertilise the land. The original village stood here, but when it became evident that the residents were more dependent on food from the mainland they moved the village to the present site of Baile Mor.

On the north of the plain, to the right of the road, is the round grassy mound of Sithean Mor "The Big Fairy Hill"; in Gaelic times it was known as Cnoc nan Aingel or "The Hill of Angels". It was here that a group of angels surrounded St. Columba while he was praying and began to speak to him. However they fled when they perceived that a brother monk was watching them.

Nearby is Bol leithne (the "Fold of Eithne") where St. Columba's spirit is said to have accompanied some monks back to the monastery after they had been harvesting.

By the jetty is the village of Martyrs' Bay where there was a massacre of sixty-eight monks by Vikings in 806. The bodies of the dead who were brought to Iona for burial were placed here upon a mound of earth called Eala. In this area is

Cladh nan Druineach which has been associated with the burial place of the skilled stone workers of Iona.

In the Secluded Hollow, at the foot of a small hill south of Dun-I, are the ruins of the Hermit's Cell; in Gaelic this was known as Cobhain Cuildich or "Culdees Cell". These were used to house the monks who preferred to live in solitude. Their bee-hive appearance is discernible. (On Eileach an Naoimh, in the Garvellochs, there are similar cells which have been associated with St. Columba. To see them you will have to hire a motor boat from Cullipool or Easdale; telephone the keykeeper at Luing 212.)

On the north slop of Dun-I, just below the summit, is the Well of Eternal Youth. It is said that if a woman bathes her face and hands in it before sunrise she will become young again. North east of the Hermit's Cell is another well where sailors, seeking favourable winds from the north threw their propitiatory offerings. Both wells are relics associated with the Druidical belief that water possesses curative and magical powers.

There is much to see on Staffa. The landing spot is called Clam Shell Cave which takes its names from the curious curvature of its basaltic columns; unfortunately the cave cannot be entered.

To the west is the Great Causeway which is similar to the Giant's Causeway in Ireland. Half-way along it is Fingal's Chair : if you sit on this rocky throne and make three wishes they will be fulfilled. To its left is an islet named Buchaille or "Herdsman"; its columns can only be seen at low tide. Try to be there when this occurs as the columns — in many cases — are horizontal, inverted or convex.

Fingal's Cave — the best known — is sixty-five feet high and two hundred and thirty feet deep. It was named after the third-century Irish hero Fionn NacCoul who the Scots called Fingal (Fionn na Ghal means Chief of Valour). It was he who defended the Hebrides against the early Viking pirates. The sides of Fingal's Cave and its ground and roof are composed of black pentagonal or hexagonal pillars; these are divided transversely by joints which are separated at two foot intervals. The cave is "musical" as harmonies are called forth by the billowing wind.

Beyond Fingal's Cave is Boat Cave : it is fourteen feet high and one hundred and fifty feet in length. It is only accessible by boat.

Further west is Mackinnon's Cave. It was named after Abbott Mackinnon of Iona who drowned off Staffa after doing penance there for an "intrigue" with Matilda of Skye. It is fifty feet high and two hundred and twenty-four feet in length.

Further west of Mackinnon's Cave is Cormorant's or Scart's Cave; its proportions are similar.

The highest point on the island is one hundred and thirty feet high and is called Meall nan Gamhna or "the rounded hill of the Stirks". A smaller hill is Meall nan Facileann or "the rounded hill of seagulls".

Be sure to see Gunna Mor (the cave with the stone in the pothole) and try to find the initials J.B. 1772 (carved by Sir Joseph Banks) two inches high on a pillar at the inner end of Fingal's Cave.

The Treshnish Isles have been called Bird Sanctuaries and, to be sure, you will find many species of sea birds nesting there. These include shags, fulmars, herring gulls, eiders, oystercatchers and puffins — to name a few. Additionally Lunga has a wide variety of flowers, one of which, the oyster plant, grows only on one of the other Treshnish Isles. Be sure to notice the ruined village on Lunga (on the north east coast) and, if you stay there, cross to the islet of Sgeir a' Chasteil on the northernmost point. Remember you have only one hour in which to do this when the water is at low tide. Other sights on the islands include the Cairn a' Burgh Beg (a ruined fort) and Cairn a' Burgh Mor (the remains of a castle). Pick out The Dutchman's Cap.

Specialised interests

Iona offers itself for study and, one can say, quite justly, that the archæologist, historian and ecclesiologist will find abundant employment on the island.

Staffa and the Treshnish Isles are "finds" for the geologist, on the one hand, and the ornithologist, on the other. It is to be hoped that more than a brief cruise around them can be made.

Further information

Events of Iona : Mull and Iona Week (12th to 18th September in 1972).

Local information

The Oban, Mull and District Tourist Organisation, Albany Street, Oban, Argyll.

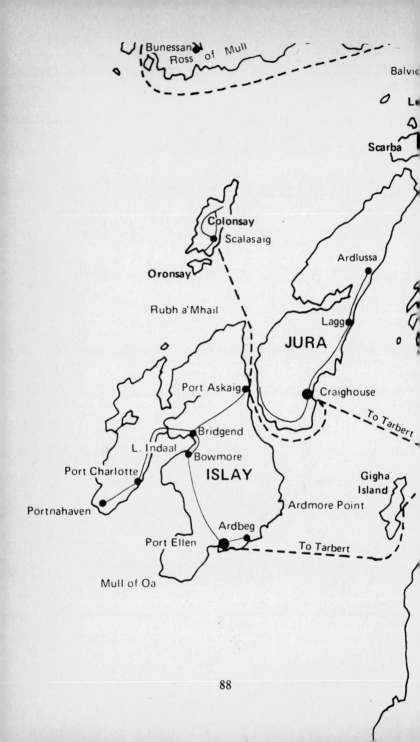

ISLAY, JURA, COLONSAY
AND ORONSAY, AND GIGHA

Description

At the southernmost end of the Inner Hebrides lay a group of islands — Islay, Jura, Colonsay and its satellite Oronsay, and Gigha — of which Islay is the centre.

To visit Islay is a heady experience, but this is not so much from the whiskey distilleries you'll find there, but rather from its excellent climate, its leisurely pace and its warm and friendly people. Islay is an island bathed in light and good cheer, an almost year round summer place filled with many charming surprises.

Twenty-five miles long and twenty-miles wide with one hundred and fifty miles of good roads, Islay can hardly be called congested, even though it boasts a population of over four thousand. It is a prosperous island, with fertile farming land and well-stocked fishing waters, a cheese factory and a number of distilleries.

At first glance it appears to be two separate islands as Loch Gruinart and Loch Indaal cut so deeply into it that the beautiful coastal Rhinns district is almost severed from the rest. In fact it is one and yet many islands all at once. Shyly competing for your attention are its many elements — its scenery, its relics from the past, its sporting areas, its bird and plant life and its delightful villages.

Here you will revel in its bays and beaches, its moors and lochs, its mountains and woods — all so lovely and so unspoiled.

Here you will find standing stones, hill forts, burial sites, ruined chapels and an abundance of carved stone work, ranging from ancient rudely-cut crosses on plain slabs to the exquisitely carved crosses of Kildalton, Kilchoman and Kilnave. For Islay is an old island, rich in a history that dates back to Neolithic times and reached a peak when it was the seat of the Lord of the Isles.

Here you can take advantage of its sporting places : its excellent eighteen-hole golf course, its fish-heavy lochs and coastal waters, its miles of silvery beaches washed by great breakers, its hills that ask to be walked on.

Here you will find birds . . .and more birds. For Islay is the home of one hundred species of bird life (ninety-seven of which were spotted there in two days in the depths of winter), and the last stronghold (with Jura) in Scotland where the chough can be seen in large numbers. Here, too, is such a wide variety of flora that the botanist will find endless delight wherever he goes on the island.

Here are attractive villages and hamlets : Bowmore, a fishing village on Loch Indaal; Port Askaig, a charming wooded hamlet on the Sound of Islay; Port Ellen, the principal village on the island; and Port Charlotte, the "capital" of the Rhinns district.

Islay is for holiday makers in the best sense of the word, for here, on Islay, you create your own holiday out of the wealth of beauty and variety it offers to you.

Jura is Islay's "sister" island — nearly as long but only eight miles wide. Like Islay it is almost two separate islands, with Loch Tarbert in the west dividing the deer forests of Ardlussa in the north from Jura forest in the south. Varied scenery is not unknown to the island—there are woods, green and gold fields, and bays of silver sand — but still the overall effect of Jura is one of great ruggedness. The contrast is sharp : one moment you can be standing near its palm trees and fuschia bushes, and the next you can find yourself face to face with its rocky coastline with its shingle-strewn foreshore which teems with all types of sea fowl. Raised beaches and caves abound, as do moorland heaths and barren or scree-covered hill slopes. But the pride of Jura is its "mountain of gold" the Beinn an Oir or, as we know them, the Paps of Jura, which reach upwards, in three peaks, to over 2,571 feet.

They are well worth the ascent, as from the top you will have a most commanding view, stretching from the Isle of Man to the Outer Hebrides. There are wild waters as well, and in the north part of the island you can see the famous and perilous Corryvreckan whirlpool which separates Jura from the neighbouring island of Scarba.

Jura's population is a mere 250, and the majority of them are employed as farmers or by the modern whiskey distillery at Craighouse, the chief village on the island. They are a hardy folk, and proof of their longevity is to be found at Ardlussa cemetery where Mary MacCrain, who died at 128, and one of her ancestors, who is reputed to have died at 180, have been laid to rest.

Jura, even less than Islay, is not an island to lay on entertainment. It does offer some facilities for the tourists, but on the whole it simply "is". There is only one main road that runs round the coast to Craighouse and on to Ardlussa and no public transport whatsoever. Cars are permitted, and tours can be taken after ferrying there from Islay. The more adventurous bring bicycles . . . or walk.

Ten miles west of Jura is Colonsay which, at low tide, is joined to the island of Oronsay. The two islands were named for St. Columba and St. Oran and together they form one parish. They share between them a population of only three hundred.

Both are islands of concentrated beauty, scenically allied to Islay and Jura. There are rocky cliffs, silver sands, many hills, picturesque bays and, in the Vale of Kiloran on Colonsay, thickly covered forest plantations. Transport, too, is largely by foot, and their many paths and tracks provide ample opportunity for the tourist to explore the more isolated areas.

The islands have much to offer to the sportsman and the specialist. Fishing is good and many big catches of mackerel, saithe and lythe have been known to have been made. In July is held Colonsay's annual Sports Event.

For the ornithologist there are ringed plovers, lesser and greater black backed gulls, oystercatchers and bar-tailed godwits — just a few of the many species of bird that inhabit the islands.

For the archæologist there are many relics of antiquity : standing stones, ruined priories and mounds or duns with

91

relics in the latter dating back to 5,000 to 7,000 B.C.

Botanists will find a wide range of flora. Certainly they must make a special visit to Colonsay's Gardens of Kiloran which house many tropical and non-tropical plants.

Geologists, too, will find much of interest in the rock formations on the islands.

Gigha is a narrow, green island, six miles long and only two miles wide. Its Norse name means "God's Island" and it was an important part of the Norse empire until the thirteenth century. It is a primitive though prosperous island, exporting potatoes, milk and lobsters to the mainland. The island has a number of interesting ecclesiastical and antiquarian remains, in addition to the sub-tropical Garden of Achamore.

History

Like most of the Hebrides the islands in this group have similar beginnings, dating back to prehistoric times up to the pre-Christian era. The islands first achieved some notoriety in 563 by being the initial landing spot for St. Columba and his followers. During the eleventh and twelfth centuries the islands were subject to the Norse invasion : Islay was particularly singled out as the island which provided the invaders with a foothold near the mainland. At this point Islay achieved some fame with the coming of the Norseman Godred Crovan: Godred is sometimes called the St. George of the Isles because of the legend that he destroyed a dragon that was laying waste to the island. His burial place is marked by the white stone or Carragh Ban near Port Ellen (see Places of Interest).

From the twelfth to the fifteenth century the islands were ruled by the Lords of the Isles, their base being a tiny island on Loch Finlaggan called Eilean Mor. From the shores one can still see the stump of their castle as well as Council Isle where the fourteen lords of the Hebrides used to meet to rule the kingdom. Allegiance was originally owed to Norway, but after 1263 it was transferred to Scotland.

After the downfall of the Lords of the Isles the history of the islands goes its separate ways. From the fourteenth to the seventeenth century Islay was governed by the Macdonald's of Dunyveg until feuds with the Macleans and intrigues between the Campbells of Argyll and King James the Sixth led to the fall of the Macdonalds (see Places of Interest) and the securing of Islay for Sir John Campbell of Calder. For about one hundred years the "Thanes of Cawdor" held Islay, and in 1726 it was sold to Daniel Campbell of Shawfield. The island had a brief renaissance until the nineteenth century but, like all other Hebridean islands, it suffered tremendously under the Clearances. Nowadays it is a prosperous island, with most of the land being owned by a small number of Lowland and English landlords.

Jura's Sound was once of strategic importance in the time of Somerled as the Lord of the Isles exacted tribute from all ships passing through. After the fall of the Macdonald's, Jura, like its sister, passed into the hands of the Campbells. They retained the island until 1938 when they sold it to five other landowners, including The Forestry Commission.

The fall of the Macdonald's on Islay also terminated the proprietorship of Colonsay and Oronsay by the MacPhees. The new owners, the Campbells, sold Colonsay in 1701 to Malcolm Mcneil of Knapdale who built Colonsay House, in 1722, from the stones of Kiloran Abbey (see Places of Interest). In 1904 Lord Strathcona bought the island and developed the Gardens of Kiloran that can still be visited today (see Places of Interest).

Prior to the battle of Largs, Gigha was one of the favourite anchorages for the Viking fleets. Under the Macdonald aegis it was ruled by the Clan Neil; like the other islands it was passed onto the Campbells of Argyll. Later in the eighteenth century, the island was sold back to the Neil family who then retained it for another century. Eventually it was bought by Colonel Sir James Horlick who, in 1945, created the woodland garden around Achamore House on the site of the two previous plantations.

How to get there

MacBraynes, as of this year, have discontinued their service to Islay, Jura, Colonsay and Oronsay, and Gigha. Western Ferries Ltd., their one-time competitors, have taken over all sailings to the islands. You can obtain their timetable from Western Ferries Ltd., Kennacraig, Tarbert (Loch Fyne), Argyll, which is also their port of embarkation.

Their service to all the islands is very frequent, and they even do Sunday sailings. In Islay you will disembark at Port Askaig; on Jura at Feolin; on Colonsay at Scalasaig; and on Gigha at its northernmost tip. An alternative way of reaching Gigha is by ferry from Tayinloan on the Kintyre coast.

Additionally BEA run frequent flights from Glasgow Airport (via Campbeltown). Islay's airport is located at Glenegedale, and from there you can take a connecting bus to the main villages on the island.

Inter- and intra-island travel

Inter-island travel has been made relatively simple by Western Ferries Ltd. There is a daily ferry service between Islay and Jura, with embarkation and debarkation at Port Askaig and Feolin. To reach Colonsay it will be necessary to go via Port Askaig on Islay as Western Ferries runs the only scheduled service there. Oronsay, as we said, can be approached on foot from Colonsay during the three hours when the sea is at low tide. Gigha can either be reached from Kennacraig on West Loch Tarbert or from Scalasaig on Colonsay or Port Askaig on Islay.

Two further side trips are possible. The first is to Scarba off the northernmost tip of Jura. The island is best approached from the mainland as then there would be less chance of being trapped in the whirlpools of Corryvreckan. The island is small, unpopulated and with many lofty cliffs.

Cara is the neighbouring island of Gigha; its population, according to the residents of Gigha, is one Brownie. Here you will find the Brownie Chair, made of stone; if you sit in it and make three wishes they are supposed to come true (see Fingal's Throne on Staffa).

Out of the group of islands only Islay has public transport; here, too, the roads are best for motoring. Jura, as we said, has only one main road. Colonsay and Oronsay and Gigha are manageable enough to see by foot or by bicycle, Islay does run some bus tours of the island; inquire about these at the Tourist Office at Bowmore.

Accommodation

As would be expected there are limited means for accommodation on some of these islands. Islay does have a number of hotels, guest houses, bed and breakfast places and cottages in both the main villages and the out of the way hamlets. There are no organised camping or caravanning sites on the island, although both are permitted on Islay Estates and Dunloissit Estates (on Islay). Particulars can be obtained from the Estates Office, Islay Estates Company, Bridgend, Islay; A. C. Macrae, Esq., Gartness House, Ballygrant, Islay; and the Tourist Offices on the mainland (Campbeltown) and on Islay itself (at Bowmore). Finally, Islay's residents will hire out caravans; prices and locations can be obtained from the aforementioned Tourist Offices.

Jura boasts one hotel and a number of bed and breakfast places and cottages. These, necessarily, are limited; their terms differ considerably. Camping is permitted, but permission should be sought.

Colonsay and Oronsay have even more restricted accommodation, with one hotel between them (on Colonsay). Camping and caravanning are *not* permitted.

Gigha has one hotel.

For additional information about accommodation write to The Mid-Argyll, Kintyre and Islay Tourist Organisation, Campbeltown, Argyllshire.

Eating facilities

None of these islands are "summer resorts" in any sense of the word and this must be borne in mind if you decide to visit them. At all of the villages there are general stores from which you can purchase your food provisions; alternatively you can either bring your food from the mainland or request full board at your hotel, guest house or bed and breakfast place.

Sport

There is much scope for sport on most of these islands.

Fishing and Sea Angling : Fishing is, perhaps, the main attraction of Islay, Jura and Colonsay. On Islay there are numerous rivers and lochs which provide excellent salmon and trout fishing. The best places to fish are Ardmore Estate, Dunloissit Estate, Islay Estates, Foreland and Rhinns of Islay Estate, Kinnabus Estate and Laggan Estate. It is important to remember, however, that fishing rights are strictly preserved and hence it will be necessary for you to obtain a licence Further details about these can be found in "Scotland for Fishing" (25p from The Scottish Tourist Board). On Jura permits can be obtained from the Craighouse Hotel to fish in the Market and Miltown loch; directions to "open" waters will also be given. On Colonsay the fishing rights for East, West and Mid-Loch Fada can be obtained at the Colonsay Hotel who own the rights to these waters.

Additionally, there is ample opportunity for sea angling off the coasts of these islands. For saithe, lythe and mackerel (and sometimes whiting and codling) the best place to go on Islay is Loch Indaal. All offshore coastal waters on Jura and Colonsay will provide much in the way of the same sort of fish. Most hotels and boarding houses on these islands are able to make arrangements for hiring boats, but be sure

...graphs by John Benton-Harris and The Scottish Tourist Board
...stone-built promontory overlooking the Lewis coastline
...ochside solitude
...e turrets of a country house in the peace of Stornoway
...eenery

1

2

3

The sun glinting off the harbourside at Stornoway, Is of Lewis.

5/9: *Colourful fishing boats moored in Stornoway harb* on the Isle of Lewis

4

5

Ready for sea: a cheerful Hebridean fisherman

Making fishing nets on Lewis - the principal industry of the isles

The calm of Stornoway harbour broken by a solitary motor-boat

6

7

8

9

10: The sun glinting off the harbourside at Stornoway, Isle of Lewis.

11: The inquisitive and wide-eyed glance of a Highland bull.

12: Highland cattle grazing in the half-light on Benbecula.

13: The serenity of the Benbecula coastline and sea-scape.

10

11

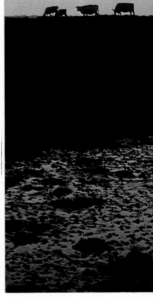

13

Ione cottage stands sentinel on Benbecula

e historical ramparts of Dunvegan Castle on the Isle of
ve

e far Cuillin stretch into an almost cloudless sky on
Isle of Skye

14

15

16

17: BEA island aircraft landing on the beach at Barra.
This airline serves 13 airports in Scotland.
18: Church on a hill - Castlebay, Barra
19: Tranquil scene on the Isle of Barra.
20: Castlebay on the Isle of Barra

17

18

21

An old life-style, crofter's cottage on Barra
A small rocky cove with clear water on Barra
Master of your own domain - here a sailing boat moored
in a cove on Barra
A fresh green landscape spanning Castlebay on Barra

22

23

24

25: *A small crofter's cottage against the ruggedly beaut[*
landscape of the Isle of Harris

26: *A fishing boat beached in a cove on the Isle of Bar[*

27: *A gorse-covered hillside on Barra Island*

28: *The unspoilt and picturesque harbourside of Tober[*
Bay, Isle of Mull

25

26

27

28

to book them in advance. There is a sea angling club at Port Charlotte on Islay.

Hillwalking and Climbing : Islay and Jura are the best for both of these sports. All of Islay's "mountains" (which include Beinn Bheigeir, Beinn Thrasda and Beinn Tart a' Mhill) are under one thousand feet and quite accessible; the views of the islands and of Jura and Colonsay are excellent. On Jura one must climb the Paps; these peaks should prove of little difficulty, even for the inexperienced. The views, as we said, are marvellous.

Golf : There is an excellent eighteen hole golf course at Machrie, Port Ellen on Islay. The main competitions are held in July and August. There are no clubs for hire but there is Sunday playing. Pitching and putting is also possible, especially on the Port Ellen Playing Fields.

Deerstalking : Jura has long been famous for her red deer. Deerstalking is available by arrangement with the Jura Hotel.

Bowling and Tennis : The Port Ellen Playing Fields (on Islay) have facilities for both bowling and tennis. Bowmore, on Islay, also has courts.

Sailing : During the season races are held by the Islay Sailing Club and the Port Ellen Regatta Club. Jura Regatta is held at Craighouse, Jura, in August, generally on the first Saturday.

Seal Spotting : Places to spot seals include Gruinart Sands on Islay, Small Isles on Jura, and Kiloran Bay on Colonsay.

Places of interest

On Islay :
Port Askaig is beautifully situated on the Sound of Jura and it is, probably, the first sight you will see when you come to Islay. A quarter of a mile away are the gardens of Dunloisset which are widely renowned for their beauty.

Loch Finlaggan, at Ballygrant, is the scene of one important part of Islay's history. Here you can see the ruined castle of Finlaggan which once belonged to the Macdonalds, the Lords of the Isles. Of particular interest are the many carved

97

stones which lie close to its now crumbling walls.

Bowmore is a large fishing village on Loch Indaal; from here you can see countless sea birds in addition to a magnificent view. In 1813 Bowmore was the scene of the rifling exploits of an American privateer.

In Bowmore there is the curious white-walled, round church of Kilarrow which dates from 1769. Legend has it that the church was built in the round so that there would be no corner in which the Devil could hide.

Port Charlotte is a pretty village and the cheese-making centre of the island. Nearby are the graves of many American soldiers who were drowned when the S.S. "Tuscania" was torpedoed offshore on the fifth of February 1918.

South of Port Charlotte is the site of one of the oldest churchyards in Islay.

Portnaven is a rocky village set on the south point of the Rhinns peninsula; it is sheltered by the small island of Orsay which has a lighthouse on it. The currents off the Portnaven coast are noted for their violence and rapidity.

From Uiskentui the road runs to Loch Gruinart. It was here that the Macdonalds, after a fierce battle, drove back the invading Macleans of Mull in 1598. Afterwards James the Sixth granted the island to Sir John Campbell of Calder as the chief of the Clan Maclean died in the fray.

At Kilchoman, beyond the beautiful Loch Gorm, is Kilchoman Church. On its grounds is one of the three Celtic crosses which exists on the island. Another is at Kilnave.

In Loch Gorm is a tiny island with a ruined castle : this was the chief objective of the battle of Gruinart in 1598.

Standing stones are not an uncommon sight on the island, there are some located near Kilchoman and others at Port Ellen, Loch Finlaggan and north of Loch Gorm. There is an interesting stone circle between Portnaven and Kilchiaran. At Kintraw the Carragh Ban (white stone) is said to mark the last resting place of a famous Norse warrior, Godred Crovan.

The area around Loch Gorm has been the scene of a number of sea disasters. Near Sanaigmore, in 1847, the emigrant ship "Exmouth" foundered with all its hands. Close to Machar Bay are the graves of those drowned when the S.S. "Otranto", carrying American troops, was lost after a collision on 6th October, 1918.

The main port of Islay is Port Ellen; here are the island's main distilleries and close by is the golf course and the airport.

To the west of the village are Kilnaughton Bay's sands, and on a small promontory there is Dunnyveg, the ruined castle of a Macdonald chieftain. The castle began its brief but tumultuous history as the objective of a clan feud; later it developed into a bone of contention between the Macdonalds and James the Sixth. In 1615 it fell into the hands of the Earl of Argyll; later it was beseiged and taken by General Leslie who cut off the water supply. In 1645 it was cast down when Colla Ciotach, who was left in command of the garrison, was seized and hung from a mast taken from his own galley.

The Oa, on the southern peninsula, has countless numbers of cliffs and caves. There are others on the island, the most famous being the great cave of Bolsa which is located four miles north west of Bonahaven. Others worth seeing are those at Slochd Mhaol Doraidh near Port Ellen and Sanaigmore. On the cliff-top of The Oa is a memorial to American servicemen lost in Machar Bay during World War I. To the south east are the remains of an entrenchment, Dun Aidh.

On the road from Port Ellen, near the hill of Cnoc, are two upright stones; these are reputed to mark the resting place of the Danish Princess Yula. The name of Islay is supposed to have been derived from her own.

At Kildalton there is a tiny church and standing before it is the thousand-year-old Cross of Kildalton. This Celtic cross is said to be one of the finest examples still in existence, rivalling those on Iona. Kildalton castle stands quite close by to the church.

From Ardtalla one can see the lighthouse on McArthur's head. Two miles inland from the Sound of Islay is Ben Bheigeir, Islay's highest mountain.

Raised beaches abound along the northern coast of Islay, and half a mile south of west Saligo Bay are some natural arches.

On Jura :

Like Islay, Jura has numerous caves, raised beaches and standing stones. The best caves of Jura are located around the mouth of Loch Tarbert, and these are among the largest and most interesting to be found in Scotland.

In the vicinity of Loch Tarbert, on the uninhabited west coast, there are many examples of raised beaches. Those at Shian Bay are more than one hundred feet above sea-level and located several hundred yards inland.

Near Jura House at Tarbert there are standing stones seven feet tall, and in the south west of the island there is the famous Camus Stack Stone which is twelve feet high and four and a half feet broad.

Finally, one must see the deer forests of Ardlussa and Jura, climb the Paps of Jura, and view the whirlpool of Corryvreckan.

On Colonsay :

The most notable attractions on Colonsay are the gardens of Kiloran. Here you will find magnificent rhododendrons, azaleas, embothriums and magnolias in addition to bamboo and palm trees.

The west coast of the island is particularly rich in raised beaches which are well worth visiting, as are the caves in the Kiloran Bay area.

The two best examples of standing stones are to be found one mile south west of Scalasaig and at the westermost tip of Loch Fada, near the hamlet of Lower Kilchatten.

In the southern part of Colonsay are the ruins of a priory, the foundations of which date back 1,400 years. Here you can see many carved stones and a cloister.

Archæologists will delight at the number of burial mounds scattered all over the island.

On Oronsay :

On the western arm of the island are the ruins of an Augustian priory, reputed to have been built on a Celtic site. The roofless church is sixty feet long and undecorated, and the adjoining cloister is straight-sided, similar to the Saxon buildings in England. In the churchyard there are two crosses. The first has its head adorned with a relief of the Crucifixion and is dated 1510. The second, and smaller, one is made up of parts of two crosses. At the prior's house there are many good sixteenth-century tomb-slabs.

On Gigha :
Here you can see the lovely gardens of Achamore with its sub-tropical plants.
Here you can also see the thirteenth century ruined church of Kilchattan with its ogam stone. A window has been dedicated to Kenneth Macleod, late pastor of the island and the author, with Marjory Kennedy-Fraser, of "The Songs of the Hebrides". Pictured are Kenneth Macleod holding a harp, surrounded by St. Columba, St. Patrick and St. Mary.

Specialised interests

From the preceding you can see that there is much on these islands for the ornithologist, archæologist, geologist and botanist.
The ornithologist would be well-rewarded by a visit to Islay, Jura and Colonsay for its wide variety of bird life.
Archæologists will find a number of ecclesiastical and non-ecclesiastical ruins on all of the islands, in addition to the numerous duns and standing stones.
The raised beaches and rock formations of the three afore-mentioned islands are of interest to the geologist. The botanist can choose between the great range of flora that adorn the countryside or are gathered together at the gardens of Dunoisset (Islay), Kiloran (Jura) and Achamore (Gigha).

Further information

Events include: Gala Day Sports and Regatta (21st July at Port Ellen, Islay); Islay, Jura and Colonsay Sheepdog Trials 24th July at Bridgend, Islay); Jura Regatta (1st August at Craighouse); Kildalton Cross Golf Tournament (3rd August at Machrie, Islay); Islay, Jura and Colonsay Agricultural Show (12th August at Bridgend, Islay); and Open Sailing Regatta (12th August at Bowmore, Islay).

Local information

The Mid-Argyll, Kintyre and Islay Tourist Organisation, Campbeltown, Argyllshire.

The Tourist Office, Bowmore, Isle of Islay.

Western Ferries Ltd., Kennacraig, Tarbert (Loch Fyne), Argyll.

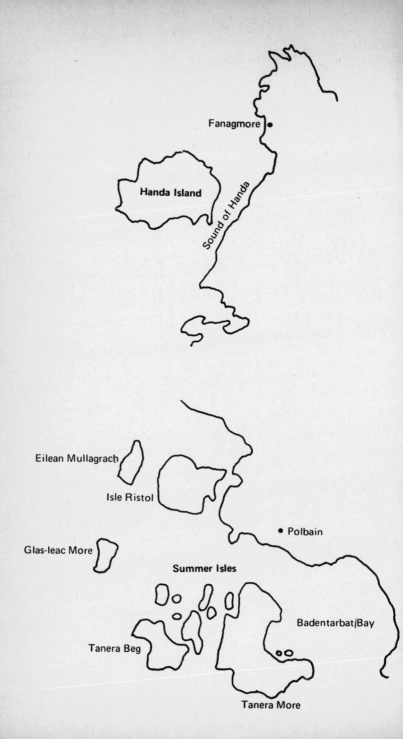

HANDA AND THE SUMMER ISLES

Description

Situated in the narrow Sound of Handa, two miles north west of the town of Scourie in Sutherland, is the island of Handa. The name itself is a corruption of the word Sandy and, to be sure, there are many sandy beaches and rabbity dunes on the south east side of the island.

But this, in fact, is not why people are drawn to it. Handa is a "feathered island", a Nature Reserve managed by The Royal Society for the Protection of Birds. Birds are the island's only inhabitants, and many of their nests are on the island's north west side which has cliffs rising some four hundred feet high. No rare species have been found on Handa — only variety and quantity.

Further south down the west coast, in Wester Ross, are a cluster of islands at the mouth of Loch Broom called the Summer Isles. Except for Tanera Mhor, the largest of the group, the islands are uninhabited. Some of the islands are used for the grazing of sheep, but most are simply breeding grounds for seals and birds. At one time some of the islands had curing stations for herring which were connected with Ullapool, but after 1820 the catches diminished acutely and the entire industry collapsed.

Tanera Mhor achieved some notoriety when Dr. Fraser Darling, the naturalist, lived there, making a comfortable home out of an uninhabited ruin. Later he wrote a book about the island called "Island Years".

Horse Island, which has a herd of wild goats, has long been known to have the best collection of bird life of all the Summer Isles.

How to get there

Access to Handa is by motor boat from the village of Tarbet, north west of Scourie. Excursions are run from the mainland, and a landing can be made on the south eastern coast. There are no boats on Sunday.

Excursions are also run to and around the Summer Isles from Ullapool or Achiltibuie; usually there is a two hour stop on Tanera Mhor.

For Handa contact the Tourist Office for Sutherland and for the Summer Isles contact the Tourist Office for Ross-shire (their addresses are listed in Local Information). You can also obtain further details locally.

Inter- and intra-island travel

Handa is four and a half miles in circumference, and the only going is by foot.

To go from one of the Summer Isles to the next you will either have to take the excursion trip or make arrangements with a local fisherman to take you to a specific island. Again the islands are small and to tour them you must go by foot.

Accommodation

Handa has, what one author called, a "five star bothy" — a refurbished cottage with accommodation for ten to twelve people (lounge and dormitory). It has a library with many materials for the naturalist, a toilet and sink in the annexe, and a fireplace (with driftwood and dry peat kept in the store-house). It is advisable to choose the bothy rather than to camp on the island. Contact The Royal Society for the Protection of Birds, 17 Regent Terrace, Edinburgh EH7 5BN or Warden, Mr A. Munro, Tarbet, Foindle by Lairg, Sutherland, for further details and permission to stay there. On Tanera Mhor the owner, who has a summer house there, is not particularly enthusiastic about campers. However, if you write to The Factor, Tanera Mhor, The Summer Isles, near Ullapool, Ross-shire, explaining your interest in the island, he may allow you to camp there. The ruined schoolhouse is usually singled out as shelter; it supposed to be rather gloomy. Bring a tent with you.

Sport

The coastal waters off the Summer Isles are excellent for sea fishing and trouting.

Eating facilities

It almost goes without saying that you must bring your food with you. The bothy on Handa does have a gas cooker, boiling rings and pots and pans.

Places of interest and specialised interests

In the main both Handa and the Summer Isles are paradises for the naturalist, but they are also places where the non-specialist, if he cares, may find new interests.

The Great Stack in the northern part of Handa is the place where the largest amount of the island's birds reside. Here and at the Little Stack (to the north east) and around the south eastern coast you will see some one hundred thousand sea fowl, including sixty thousand guillemots, four thousand fulmars, five hundred shags, twelve thousand razorbills and eight hundred puffins, to name a few. There is a footpath which is located to the west of the bothy and from here you can take a direct route to the Great Stack. Climb the cliffs as from here you will have a magnificent view of the mainland.

Also of interest is the ruined village at the foot of the Great Stack and the old burial ground just above Port an Eilein in the south eastern part of the island. According to L. R. Higgens it was once "the custom to bury the dead on the island in order that the remains could lie peacefully, undisturbed by foraging wolves". The gravestones should be quite old as the island was evacuated in 1846.

The Summer Isles have been described by the same author as "a self-contained Highland of Scotland", and, necessarily, there is that strange combination of the barren, the rocky and the flower strewn (including, here, wild flowers, purple orchis, forget-me-nots, foxgloves and more). The highest precipice on Tanera Mhor is Meall Mhorr which reaches upwards of four hundred feet.

There is a certain amount of gloom on the island and there are remains of the once-prosperous life there, including the village with the schoolhouse, the pub and the disused fish factory. There is also a burial ground. Tanera Berg, which is close by and can be seen on the excursion trip, is a much more cheerful island with bays, green terraces and cliffs.

From almost every spot on the island you can see other Summer Isles and islets; one, Eilean na Saille is one hundred yards off the west coast and is accessible by foot at low tide. If you stand on the Anchorage on the eastern side of Tanera Mhor you have an excellent view of the coast with its cliffs, bays and tiny caves.

Birds on Tanera Mhor are not abundant, but there is a wide variety of them, including colonies of shags, fulmars, guillemots, divers and eiders. You will definitely fare better on Horse Island — if you can gain access.

Local information

Sutherland Tourist Organisation, The Square, Durnoch, Sutherland (there is an Information Office at Lairg).
Wester Ross Tourist Organisation, Sands Estate, Gairloch, Wester Ross.

Butt of Lewis
Port of Ness
Dell
Ness
Cellar Head
Borve
Muirneag
Barvas
Tolsta Head
North Tolsta
Carloway
Shawbost
Back
Broad Bay
Gallan Head
Great
Bernera
Newmarket
Tiumpan
Portnaguira
Uig
Callanish
Stornoway
Melbost
L. Roag
LEWIS
Bayble
Chicken Head
Aird Brenish
Crossbost
Loch
Balallan
Cromore
Langavat
L. Erisort
Kintaravay
Scarp
Gravir
Kebock Head
N. Harris
Park
Husinish
Ardvourlie
Castle
L. Shell
HARRIS
Ardhasig
Taransay
Tarbert
L. Seaforth
Toe Head
S. Harris
Scalpay
Shiant
Islands
Scarastovore
Pabbay
Leverburgh
Berneray
Rodel
Renish Point

To Kyle of Lochalsh

To Uig

110

THE OUTER HEBRIDES

LEWIS AND HARRIS

Description

Lewis and Harris are commonly believed to be two separate islands, but in fact they are one — firmly attached to each other by a land-breadth of some fourteen miles. However, as if to demonstrate their separateness, Lewis has been assigned to the County of Ross and Cromarty while Harris belongs to Inverness-shire.

Lewis is the larger, measuring thirty miles in length and averaging fourteen miles in width. It is also, by far, the most prosperous of the two, with its colourful capital Stornoway supporting a population of well over five thousand, mainly in the fishing and weaving industries. Lewis is a low-lying island, very flat in parts and quite barren, though not throughout. Harris is more rugged — if not more beautiful — with a variety of scenery that ranges from moonscape to moorland to beaches and to peaks which reach upwards of 2,500 feet. Time literally does stand still on these islands, but Harris is decidedly the "sleepier" of the two.

Both Lewis and Harris are Gaelic outposts, culturally and in speech, and the vibrancy of their people results from their weird and wild individuality, their conservative-anarchist streak, their hardiness and hospitableness and their extreme volubility. The Gaels of these islands are more than just

friendly folk : they are warm, likeable and very much alive
To be sure they have their eccentricities, their cautiousness
and their suspiciousness, but they respond to you if you are
simply honest with them.

The economy of the islanders is one of well-developed
peasantry in the best sense of the word. Lewis has much more
of a foothold in the twentieth century and Stornoway is its
example of island life become "modern". Here you will find
a working community : a seaport that services not only local
fishing boats and steamers, but also a great number of foreign
luxury liners. A market town and a manufacturing centre.
Stornoway contains a variety of industries : those connected
with fishing (kippers and scampi in particular) and those
connected with clothing, including the making of hand-knitted
garments and the famous hand-woven Harris Tweed (more
tweed is in fact woven on Lewis than on Harris). In a sense
it is a town with elements of city-life : there are a number of
fine (licensed) hotels, a supermarket, a secondary school and
college, good restaurants and cafes, shops and a cinema.

Many of the island's sporting facilities are concentrated in
Stornoway, and the town itself has an eighteen-hole golf
course, facilities for bowling, tennis and putting, parks and
areas for skin diving, dinghy sailing, canoeing and water ski-
ing. A swimming pool is now under construction, as is a
community centre. Fishing and sea-angling are excellent, both
in Stornoway and its environs, and Stornoway itself even has
a Sea Angling Club. There are over twenty-five beautiful
beaches to choose from on the island and most of the bays
are safe to bathe in.

Ancient monuments can be found in many parts of the island,
with Lewis' long history being reflected in the famous Standing Stones of Callanish, which rivals Stonehenge, and the dun
at Duncarloway, among the finest examples of the Pictish
broch. There are, additionally, a number of fine chapels and
other ecclesiastical sights.

Harris is the "less developed" of the two islands, and consequently its appeal is of another sort, but nonetheless
satisfying.

The existence of so much mountainous area has made Harris
a favourite spot for climbing. Here you can climb the numerous steep cliffs with their remarkable bird life (which also

abounds on Lewis) and the mountains of Clisham (the highest in the Outer Hebrides). Fishing and sea angling are good to excellent, and the Harris Sea Angling Club has competitions one evening a week throughout the summer months. There are many beaches, all of them clean and the majority of them deserted, with bays that are safe for bathing and strong waves that are fine for surfing.

Here, too, are relics from the past : duns at Rodel and Borve, black houses and standing stones. The Chapel at Rodel, St. Clement's, must be seen as must the ancient chapel at Toe Head. There is a castle too, a magnificent building that was erected in the last century.

Tarbet is the main town in Harris, and although it does not offer as many amenities as Stornoway, it is very picturesque and quite gay. Much of the population resides in scattered villages and hamlets, with crofting as their main occupation. As their income is small, most people on Harris engage in subsidiary employment, and such traditional crafts as handweaving knitwear and tweed have been recently augmented by shell craft and wood turning, and the making of fancy goods out of sealskin.

Harris is also an excellent jumping off spot for visiting the islands within its boundaries. Scarp, the Shiant Islands, Taransay, Bernera, Pabbay and Shillay can all be reached by hired boats, making an excellent afternoon's outing, or more.

History

The history of Lewis and Harris is, with only a few departures, totally in line with the history of the other Hebridean islands. Like these islands, Lewis and Harris suffered much from the Viking invasion : there are still remnants of Norse words being used, especially on Lewis. Both islands' leaders claimed kinship through Olave the Black, Viking King of

Man and The Hebrides, who won his throne some seven hundred and forty years ago. Later the Macleods took control of these islands, ruling them from his castle on Skye. In 1779 they passed out of his hands, and it was not until Lord Leverhulme arrived after the First World War, were the two islands, then held as separate estates, reunited.

Again, like many of the Hebridean islands, Lewis and Harris were touched on by Bonnie Prince Charlie. Near Kyles Scalpay in Harris the Prince found refuge in the home of the farmer Donald Campbell, then on the site which the Free Church now stands.

The Clearances wrecked havoc with the islands, severely depopulating them and ruining their economy. The problem of croft division hit these islands quite hard and the poaching of their waters by foreign trawlers ruined much of their fishing industry. The efforts of the Department of Agriculture and the Highlands and Islands Development Board Scheme (see History in the Introduction) have done much to buttress their economy, but it is the spirit of the islanders themselves, particularly on Lewis, which has given impetus to industry. Indeed, many of the Lewis-men who learn their trades on the mainland return to the island and set themselves up in Stornoway.

Lord Leverhulme purchased the islands in 1918 and endeavoured, and in the end unsuccessfully, to influence their economy. Although he was extremely fond of the islands and their people, he took a rather pragmatic (some say dreamy) view of their wilting economy. His main scheme was to put the fishing and farming industries back on their feet and to market their produce throughout the world. To this end factories were built and what is now known as Leverburgh in Harris, was created. Some say he was defeated by the islanders who were suspicious of his regimentation and who supported, instead, the ex-servicemen who took more active steps to retain the land. Others say that he was frustrated by the Department of Agriculture and resented all governmental interference. In any case he died defeated, leaving the Lewis men Stornoway, its cattle and Lady Lever Park.

Since Lord Leverhulme's attempt the islanders have made economic advances. Certainly the growth of tourism has been of much help.

How to get there

With Lewis and Harris we are back to MacBraynes. There is a frequent direct car ferry service between the Kyle of Lochalsh and Stornoway; the journey takes a little over six hours. During the summer there is a frequent car ferry service to Tarbert on Harris via Uig on Skye.

BEA run a twice-daily service from Glasgow and a daily flight from Inverness to Stornoway. Loganair provide a daily flight from Stornoway to Glasgow and also offer charter services. Peregrine Air Service also operate charter services.

For timetables and flight schedules contact MacBraynes, BEA and Loganair. Peregrine's address is Peregrine Air Service, Dalcross Airport, Inverness.

Inter- and intra-island travel

For the larger islands where you will want to take your car you must use the services of MacBraynes. To reach Uig on Skye you can take a MacBraynes car ferry from Tarbert on Harris; from there you can catch another boat which will transport you to Lochmaddy on North Uist. To reach Barra from Tarbert, again with a car, go to Uig then Lochmaddy and from there drive through North Uist, Benbecula and South Uist. At Lochboisale there is a car ferry service to Barra. To reach the mainland you will have to go back to Lochboisdale and take a car ferry to Mallaig.

Simpler means to large island-hopping are possible, but for these you will have to relinquish the use of your car (though not your motor-cycle or bicycle). (Car hire, though limited, can be done in some of the larger centres.) To reach North Uist from Lewis and Harris, go to Leverburgh on Harris and take a motorboat across the sea to Newton Ferry on North Uist. As there isn't any bus service to Newton Ferry hire a taxi to take you to Lochmaddy. From there you can take a bus through the three islands and catch the regular steamer service to Barra.

There is much in the way of small isle hopping from Lewis and Harris, and this could prove to be quite fun.

Just south west of the Butt of Lewis, the northernmost point on the island, is the isle of Luchburan, sometimes known as the "Isle of Little Pigmies" or "Pigmies' Isle". The island itself is a mere twenty feet wide and eighty feet long. From the sixteenth century it has long been supposed that the island was inhabited by pigmies who arrived at Ness in 500 B.C. and were driven to the island some five hundred years later. Some believe they were of Spanish origin. There is much speculation about the size of the inhabitants of the island. Bones have been found that are rather small and there is a division of opinion about whether these were human or animal remains. Those who place their case for "pigmies" look to the church that was unearthed there. It has two un-rooted chambers, one circular and the other oblong, connected by a passage. The entire structure is, naturally, built lengthwise and is only twenty-five feet. Others who opt for animals claim that the island was used by normal sized hermits; these dismiss the church as the circle of what is suspected to be tiny huts. Judge for yourself !

Also off the coast of Lewis are the Flannon Islands or the "Severn Hunters". The largest of these does contain the remains of hermits' cells. They are visited half-yearly by a boat from Callanish. In 1900 they were the scene of tragedy as the three lighthouse keepers disappeared from there without a trace.

Thirty miles north of the Butt of Lewis is the Isle of Sula Sgeir. Once a year the fishermen visit the island to catch the young solan goose or gugas which they regard as a delicacy. The island and its neighbour North Rona are Nature Reserves.

From Callanish on the west coast of Lewis you can walk across a bridge to the island of Bernera. The island is one of the main lobster-fishing areas on or near Lewis and it contains a number of fine lochs for fishing.

Other islands off Lewis that can be visited with some ease are the Isle of Berisay, once the retreat of the outlawed Neil

Macleod (take a boat from Uig) and Eilean Calum Chille or St. Columba's Isle, which contains the remains of a church of the same name and an old graveyard (take a boat from Cromore). Finally Rona, which is owned by Alex MacFarquhar, could be seen. It lies thirty-five miles off the Port of Ness and is uninhabited except for seals and sheep.

Harris boasts a number of satellite islands. The best known is Scalpay which is across the Kyles Scalpay from Tarbert. MacBraynes run a scheduled car ferry service to the island. It has a population of five hundred, most of whom make their living from fishing activities, mainly herring and lobster.

Further out by ten miles are the Shiant Islands, magnificent by virtue of their enormous cliffs which are the home of thousands of sea birds. Hiring a boat for a trip there is not that simple as the seas can be rough; the best place to do it, though, is on Scalpay.

Compton MacKenzie was once the owner of these islands, but in 1937 he sold them to Nigel Nicolson. Camping is permitted on Eilean an Tighe ("Isle of the House") which is connected, at low tide, to Garbh Eilean. Eilean an Tighe does, in fact, have a derelict bothy which contains two rooms, a fireplace, concrete flooring and a red-painted roof. There is a tiny bit of furniture inside and, unfortunately, an abundance of flies and rats, Its mark of civilization is a visitor's book. The last inhabitant of the island was a woman who left at the beginning of the century, after the death of her father. Some very romantic and tragic stories are connected with her. It was reputed, in the 1960s, that she was living in Tarbert. On the island you can see the ruins of a church dedicated to the Virgin Mary and a number of ruined cottages. Sheep are in evidence as the island is let for grazing. On both islands there is a wide variety of sea birds and flowers.

Off the coast at Hushinish is the island of Scarp. The last island family left only recently, but some young craftsmen from Inverness have taken their place. Here, too, the cliffs harbour many sea birds, including fulmars, shags and black guillemots.

Off Harris' south east coast is a group of islands clustered in the Sound of Harris. The largest is Bernera; it is the only one to support a population. Here you can find many sandy beache, boats, attractive thatched houses and more. The usual approach is from Lochmaddy on North Uist.

At the west end of the Sound of Harris is the island of Pabbay which, at one time, had three hundred and fifty people and a whiskey industry. The Clearances destroyed it. Next to Pabbay is Shillay where, in autumn, large numbers of seals congregate. Camping on Pabbay (with permission) is possible. Look out for the ruins of a church and a grave-yard.

Finally off the town of Scarista is the large island of Taransay. Once it was a well populated island but now it is simply used as a large farm.

The majority of these islands are on the unscheduled inter-island ferry service. For a complete listing of operators send for details from The Western Isles Tourist Organisation, South Beach Quay, Stornoway, Isle of Lewis. Reservations can be made at the individual Tourist Offices (their addresses are listed in Local Information) or on the spot.

Returning to the islands themselves, Lewis and Harris do have a scheduled bus service. Highland Omnibuses Ltd. cover both islands and also does day tours from Stornoway to Rodel. Additionally a company called Mitchell's and Western Lewis Coaches Ltd. service Lewis solely. A list of their schedules *should* be obtained before you start on your tour of the islands as you may find yourself stranded. There is no Sunday service; keep this in mind. Contact The Western Isles Tourist Organisation (address is given above). Finally, when you reach an area which has a Tourist Office be sure to go in and re-check your information; sometimes there are changes in the schedules as a bus breaks down.

Accommodation

Lewis and Harris might seem to some to be "the ends of the earth" and completely without accommodation facilities; this is not at all true. Lewis, in fact, offers a wide range of facilities, including a number of hotels, cottages, guest houses and bed and breakfast places. To a lesser degree so does Harris. In both cases you must book ahead as, while accom-modation exists, it is still somewhat limited.

Camping and caravanning are also possible on these islands, and both of them offer caravans for hire. Charges are very reasonable. Locations include Stornoway, Crossbost, Carloway and Borve on Lewis and Tarbert, Drinishader and Scarista on Harris.

There is a youth hostel on Harris, located near Loch Seaforth, at Renigidale. It has been called "the smallest and certainly the most remote hostel in Britain"; they're not joking.

Additionally there is some accommodation on a few of the satellite islands we mentioned previously. These include, either solely or in combination, cottages, guest houses and caravans on Berneray, Scalpay, Bernera and Scarp.

For details write to The Western Isle Tourist Organisation.

Eating facilities

Both Stornoway and Tarbert offer the visitor a number of restaurants and cafes. In the more secluded villages and hamlets an evening meal is offered along with bed and breakfast. The charge is minimal and the food is plentiful. For snacks most of the towns have a general store; a few have cafes. Lewis, especially, has vans with food, a special bonus to campers, caravanners and those who frequent hostels. If you're lucky, you can also buy fresh fish from the delivery trucks. For those who decide to camp on the islands off shore, be certain that you take enough food and water.

Sport

We have already mentioned that Lewis and Harris have many excellent sporting facilities, and for many this is the sole reason why they holiday there.

Fishing and Sea Angling : Lewis and Harris' lochs and coastal waters are fish plentiful — it is as simple as that ! Salmon and brown trout predominate, but there are also a few other sorts mixed in. In Stornoway and environs one should fish at the following lochs : Airigh nan Gleann, Beag a' Ghrianain, Mor a' Ghrianain, Breughach, Beag na Chaoibhe and Leiniscall (from the Stornoway to Tarbert Road); Airigh na Lic, a' Bhuna and an Eilein (from the Uig Road); and Mor a' Chocair and Vatandip (from the Pentland Road). In Harris you should try West Loch Tarbert, the Laxdale lochs (ask for permission from the Harris Hotel), and in lochs off the three roads that run into the Tarbert-Rodel Road in the small harbour at Rodel.

Stornoway is now regarded as one of the foremost sea angling centres in Scotland, but angling itself is much in evidence in all the coastal waters off both of the islands. In these one can catch cod, haddock, whiting, saithe, pollack, gurnard, skate, mackerel, dabs, flounder, halibut, dogfish, plaice, conger, wrasse and turbot. Details about angling can be obtained from The Western Isles Tourist Association; from the Secretaries of the Stornoway Sea Angling Club, South Beach Quay, Stornoway, Isle of Lewis and the Harris Sea Angling Club, Tarbert, Isle of Harris; and from The Scottish Tourist Board (ask for "Scotland for Fishing" and "Scotland for Sea Angling" — 25p and 20p respectively). Both clubs have boats for hire and both of them run evening expeditions. Membership is not necessary.

In 1967 Stornoway was the scene of the International Team Championship and the Scottish (Open) Boat Championships; nearly 3,600 pounds of fish were landed at this festival. By popular request Stornoway is again to be used for the festival; the dates are the 27th to the 29th of September in 1972.

Hillwalking and Climbing : Lewis, as we noted, is fairly flat and hence it can't be regarded strictly as walking country. Harris, on the other hand, is hilly and there are a number of mountains that could be attempted. These include the highest peak, Clisham, which is 2,622 feet, and the lesser peaks which surround it; the hills around Loch Voshimid and along East Loch Tarbert; the mountains of Beinn on Teanga, Ben Luskentyre (from here you can see St. Kilda, an island discussed in a later chapter) and more.

Golf : Stornoway sports an eighteen hole golf course. Clubs are for hire; there is no Sunday playing. Throughout the summer there are a wide variety of competitions and this year Lewis' Golf week is to be held from the 8th of July to the 15th of July. Further details can be obtained from The Western Isles Tourist Organisation. For entry forms for matches write to Mr I. M. Cumming, Match Secretary, Stornoway Golf Club, 10 Matheson Road, Stornoway, Isle of Lewis.

Bowling, Tennis and Putting : Close to the Golf Club are a number of facilities for these sports.

Sailing and Water Ski-ing : The Sailing Club of Stornoway presently has about six dinghies which can be used by experienced sailors. Contact the club secretary upon arrival at Stornoway 335. Also available is water ski-ing which is frequently done in the evenings at Loch Airidh na Lic (two miles from Stornoway) and sometimes in Stornoway Harbour. Telephone Stornoway 303 or 903 for information.

Swimming and Surfing : There are twenty-five beaches alone on Lewis and almost a comparable amount on Harris. The waters off shore are excellent for wading, swimming and, sometimes, for surfing. Details of locations and directions can be obtained from The Western Isles Tourist Organisation.

Places of interest

On Lewis :

In Stornoway itself you should see the plaque commemorating Lewis' famous sons (located at the Town Hall); the tablet at Martin's Memorial Church, which marks the birthplace of Alexander Mackenzie of Luskentyre, the discoverer of the Mackenzie River; the prayer book and red granite font brought by Livingstone from the Flannan Isles and now on view at St. Peter's Church.

For those interested in schools, there are The Nicolson Institute — the only secondary school in the Outer Hebrides — and The Lewis Castle College — where navigation, textiles and building are taught. The Castle was built over a century ago, and is located in a rather picturesque spot in the town. In 1925 it was presented by Lord Leverhulme to Stornoway's residents, in addition to the surrounding Lady Lever Park.

At the entrance to Stornoway's harbour is a monument to Bonnie Prince Charlie who was frustrated in his attempts to buy a boat at Stornoway. On the other side of the harbour is a rock which is known as "The Beasts of Holm". It was here, on New Year's Day in 1919, that the Admiralty yacht "Iolaire" was sunk, with two hundred soldiers and sailors returning home from the war drowning in sight of the shore.

If possible, take a tour of one of the weaving mills of Stornoway. Raw Scottish wool is shipped to them in bales where it is prepared for dyeing, blending, carding, spinning and hand warping. Lorries then take the spun yarn to crofters throughout the island who weave it into cloth. You can see bundles of tweed lying by the side of the road, waiting for lorries to pick them up again. Shops throughout the Hebrides sell both the cloth and wool in addition to the finished products of Harris Tweed and sweaters. At present there are over 5,000 designs to choose from.

Uig Chapel and cemetery stand on the shores of Broad Bay at the east end of Braighe Sands. The chapel, which is now in ruins, was at the time of the Reformation one of two priories in the Western Isles; the other is at Rodel in Harris. It is said that the chapel was founded by one of the Macleod chiefs in honour of St. Catan. Here you can see an armed effigy of Roderick Macleod, famous in the time of James the Second. On the north side is a beautiful Celtic stone commemorating Margaret Macleod, the mother of the last Abbot of Iona. Here too are buried the Fifth Earl of Seaforth and Colin Mackenzie; the latter was the First Surveyor General of India. In 1828 the last service was held in the chapel. The last person to be buried in the chapel was Margaret Macleod of Bayble. No one is certain why she was buried there.

Near Portvoller is Tiumphead Head Lighthouse which was visited by the present Prince Charles on the Royal Tour of the Western Isles; he inaugurated the foghorn.

At Bragar there is a rather astounding sight : clamped to the two ends of a gatestone is an enormous whalebone arch standing straight up; from it hangs the harpoon which killed the whale.

Nearby is the village of Arnol which is sometimes called "Little Holland" because it has stone dykes. Open to the public is a preserved black house or tigh dubh. At Shawbost one can see the remains of an ancient meal mill and a new Harris Tweed spinning and finishing mill.

At Ballanthrushal, in the Ness District, is the "Thrushel Stone", a monolith standing twenty feet tall. On the moor to the east stands the stone circle and cairn of Steinacleitt.

Further out on the cape of the Butt of Lewis is a lighthouse, surrounded by impressive cliffs and rock pinnacles which are studded with sea fowl. Here, too, is the Church of St. Moluag; St. Moluag Christianised Lismore in the sixth century but was not included in the community of Irish Celtic saints (see Lismore in Inter- and Intra-Island Travel in the chapter on Mull). The church was built in the twelfth century and is also known as the Teampull Mhor. It is owned by the Scottish Episcopal Church who still hold services there.

Duncarloway, a village not too far from Shawbost, was so named because of the dun or Pictish fort which stands on a hill nearby. The tower is circular and thirty feet high; crude internal stairs have been made out of unhewn stone. At Shawbost there is a folk museum.

One of the most elaborate and most perfect megalithic temples in Britain is in the village of Callanish. The circle of stones, which is forty feet in diameter, contains, at one end, a three-part cairn and a monolith which stands eighteen feet tall. Radiating from the circle are single or double rows of stones, in the form of a cross. A quarter and a half mile away from this site are two lesser stone circles.

At Kinlochresort can be found the remains of "beehive" houses.

Finally, around the head of Loch Erisort is the famous Deer Forest with its small herds of red deer. The scenery is the best one can find on Lewis.

On Harris :

In North Harris one should see Amhuinnsuidhe Castle, built in the last century by the Earl of Dunmore. The stones were imported to the island and the entire effect is one of warmth and grace.

Close by is the hydro-electric dam on Loch Chliostair; it was the first arch dam constructed in the Western Isles.

The area around the castle is well known for its beautiful lochs and the wild red deer which live on the hills. The rivers here have abundant salmon and trout.

In Loch Voshimid there is a tiny island which, some say, served as an inspiration for Barrie when he wrote "Mary Rose".

At Glen Laxdale there are a number of examples of funeral cairns, built where coffin bearers rested their burden on their way to the graveyards at Luskentyre.

At the south east end of the island is Glass Island Lighthouse and from here you have a magnificent view of the islands in the Outer Hebrides, Skye and even bits of the mainland.

At Rodel, on the southern tip of Harris, is the wonderful Church of St. Clement. It has a sturdy square tower with some excellent sculpture. The church was built in the sixteenth century by Alasdair Crottach Macleod, chief of the Macleods of Harris and Dunvegan in Skye. The church contains the stately tomb in which he was buried in 1547, in addition to other. It is believed that the same stone that was taken from Mull and used in the building of Iona Cathedral also found its way here. In the graveyard is the tomb of Donald Macleod of Berneray who fought for Prince Charles at Falkirk and who sired nine children after his marriage (the third) at seventy-five.

Also at Rodel and at Borve are the remains of duns.

Toe Head, on the west coast of South Harris is worth a visit, not only for its cliffs which provide a nesting place for sea birds, but also for its ancient chapel. Little is known about this chapel, but it is generally assumed that it was built at the same time as St. Clement's.

Along the coast one should see (and climb) Chaipaval, which is only 1,200 feet and which gives an excellent view of the surrounding islands, and Ben Seilebost, a perfect spot for the bird-watcher.

Borve Lodge, at Scarista, was the home of Lord Leverhulme when he was in Harris. There is a small woodland in this area which was planted by the Earl of Dunmore.

At the headland, near Glett Nisabost, is a huge standing stone that stands like a sentinel. From time to time the remains of earth houses and cairns are revealed among the sand dunes near the shore.

Ben Luskentyre's steep cliffs which overlook West Loch Tarbert are the haunt of the raven and the golden eagle. At times you can see small herds of red deer in the vicinity.

Specialised interests

Bird life abounds on Lewis and Harris as do flowering plants and various rocks. If possible, however, the ornithologist, botanist and geologist should take a trip to Scarp or to North Rona and Sula Sgeir. For the latter, which contains rocks of Lewisian gneiss, forty-three flowering plants and a variety of birds, contact Hon. Warden, Mr James MacGeoch, 67 Milton Park, Aviemore, Inverness-shire and he will send you information on the islands which are now Nature Reserves. Archæologists would do well to visit the various duns on the islands and, of course, the Callanish Standing Stones.

Further information

Events on Lewis and Harris include : Lewis Provincial Mod. (14th to 16th June in 1972); Lewis Golf Week (8th to 15th July); Lewis Carnival (14th of July to 5th August); Harris Gala Week (21st July to 28th July); North Harris Agricultural Show and Sheep Dog Trials (2nd of August); South Harris Agricultural Show (10th August); Western Isles (Open) Sea Angling Championship (17th and 18th of August at Stornoway); and The Scottish (Open) Boat and International Sea Angling Championships (27th to 29th September at Stornoway).

Local information

The Western Isles Tourist Organisation, South Beach Quay, Stornoway, Isle of Lewis.
Tourist Information Centre, Pier Road, Tarbert, Isle of Harris.

NORTH UIST,
BENBECULA AND SOUTH UIST
AND SURROUNDING ISLANDS

Description

To the south-west of Lewis and Harris, and further along the "Long Chain", are the islands of North Uist, Benbecula and South Uist. Previously separated, the islands are now linked together by causeways.

The islands, though in many ways similar, do have individual differences. North Uist betrays a much more Nordic flavour, while the islands to its south are more overtly Gaelic. The entire population of North Uist is Protestant whereas ninety-five per cent of the inhabitants of South Uist are Catholic. Benbecula's residents are evenly divided between the two religions.

North Uist played little if any part in the wanderings of Bonnie Prince Charlie; Benbecula, South Uist and its satellite Eriskay have many associations with his plight, particularly through their "native daughter", Flora Macdonald.

Of this group of islands South Uist is definitely the more prosperous, though the others are making some headway into industrial schemes.

North Uist has been called "an island of contrasts" and this is indeed, quite true. Along the eastern shores of the island are many high hills (in particular Eaval and South Lee), undulating moors and innumerable trout-filled lochs. Along the west coast the scenery is lush, with mile upon mile of rolling verdant land, fertile with crops and filled with wild flowers. Here, too, are silvery beaches that stretch as far as the eye can see and whose off-shore waters are safe for swimming and surfing.

Not only is North Uist a paradise for the angler, the hill-walker and the swimmer, but also it is a veritable treasure trove for the archæologist. The island is fairly filled to over-flowing with stone circles, cairns, duns and forts, many of which are in the area of Newton Ferry. The reminders of its past are plentiful and throughout you can see wheel houses, black houses, ruined chapels and old cemeteries.

The ornithologist and the botanist are very well provided for both on the island and off its shores. Along the west coast sea fowl and wild flowers are much in abundance, and there are Nature Reserves at Balranald and on the Monach Islands.

North Uist, particularly, is an island with many satellites which stud the seas like so many seals. Here you have the islands and islets of Berneray, Pabbay, Boreray — to name a few — some of them still inhabited while others are not. Almost all of them contain some relic of the past or some spot where there is a curiosity of nature. A few are tidal islands and you can cross to them when there is low tide.

Sandwiched between the Uists is the low-lying island of Benbecula which is frequently known as the "Mountain of the Fords". In many respects it shares some of the best features of its sister islands : there are delightful meadows, moors, dunes and beaches with numerous lochs that provide excellent fishing. There are ruins as well and many of the island lochs have duns nearby. To the east are a maze of tiny islands which are notable for being the landing spot of Bonnie Prince Charlie. Here, too, is Balivanich Airport which is serviced by Stornoway, Glasgow and Inverness.

South Uist is a rugged island with as many, if not more, contrasts per mile than its northern neighbours. Here is an island of tall mountains and of flower-spangled machair beside beautiful white sandy beaches. Here, too, are three fjord-like indentations on the east coast which form the picturesque anchorages of Loch Skipport, Loch Eynort and Lochboisdale, the latter being the main village and port.

Like North Uist this island possesses an abundance of sites of archæological interest, with numerous cairns, wheel houses and ruined chapels. Loch Druidebeg and the three hundred and sixty five islands in its waters is a celebrated Nature

Reserve, and the most important feeding ground in Britain for the grey lag goose. Some of the islands are covered with a thick undergrowth and stunted trees, while on others the royal fern grows plentifully. On the north side of the loch there is a large plantation of rhododendrons. Herons abound. South Uist is a sporting island, and its one hundred and ninety lochs are filled with trout and salmon. Its beaches are extensive and there is bathing, swimming and surfing in the coastal waters. South Uist also contains a golf course and shooting areas.

South Uist, too, is an island with a firm toe-hold in the twentieth century, although its modern (and controversial) Rocket Range does contrast strongly with the old cottages of the nearby village of Geirinish.

History

The history of the Uists and Benbecula in the main resembles the history of the other islands in the Hebrides. Accordingly they suffered from plundering Vikings, the fierce wars between the clans, and the Clearances of the nineteenth century. Their brief moment came with the appearance of Bonnie Prince Charlie who literally put Eriskay on the map by first stepping foot onto it when he entered Scotland. Flora Macdonald, who was born on South Uist, here became instrumental in helping the Prince cross to Benbecula and from thence over the seas and islands to Skye.

How to get there

MacBraynes have a car ferry service from Mallaig to Lochboisdale on South Uist. Alternatively you can go from the Kyle of Lochalsh to Portree on Skye and from there drive or take a bus to Uig and cross by car ferry to Lochmaddy on

North Uist. The service is quite frequent during the summer: details can be obtained from MacBraynes.

If you wish to go by air, BEA and Loganair have a twice-daily service from Glasgow and a daily flight from Inverness to Balivanich Airport on Benbecula. From there you can take a bus to either of the Uists. These flights do not operate on Sunday. Contact BEA and Loganair for further details.

Inter- and intra-island travel

Of all the Hebridean islands, the Uists and Benbecula have a great deal of scope for visiting nearby islands.

The four main islands to visit from here are Skye, Lewis and Harris, and Barra. To reach Uig on Skye simply take a car ferry from Lochmaddy on North Uist. To reach Harris (and consequently Lewis) without having to return to Skye, rent a motorboat from Newton Ferry (in the northern end of North Uist); this will take you to Leverburgh on Harris. To reach Barra you can either take the MacBraynes steamer from Lochboisdale on South Uist or hire a boat to take you across the waters. There is an air connection between Balivanich Airport on Benbecula and Stornoway Airport on Lewis. Further details about these can be obtained from MacBraynes, BEA, Loganair and The Western Isles Tourist Organisation.

From North Uist :

Newton Ferry is the jumping off point for the islands of Berneray, Pabbay and Boreray (see Inter- and Intra-Island Travel on Lewis and Harris). The first island supports a heavy population, the majority of them lobster fishermen and sheep farmers. The second is uninhabited and is also known as Priests' Island. Tradition has it that the former inhabitants were found guilty of illicit distilling of whiskey and were evacuated as a result of it. Borerary still has one family living on it.

Opposite Sollas is the beautiful little island of Vallay. On it stands a mansion that was built by Erkine Beveridge, who wrote the book "Archeology and Topography of North Uist".

At present the mansion (as well as the North Uist Estate) is owned by Earl Granville, a cousin of Queen Elizabeth.

Situated in Loch Scolpaig is the islet of Scolpaig. The islet is noted for its natural arches on the seaward slope of Ben Scolpaig and for its dun (a miniature castle) which was erected by Dr Alexander Macleod, chamberlain of the Macdonald estates and also (if not better) known to the islanders as "An Dotair Ban". Similar edifices can be seen on Skye at Uig and overlooking Portree Bay. On a clear day the islands of the St. Kilda group are plainly visible.

Off the coast of Kilpheder are the islands of Haisgeir and Hasgeir Eagach. The latter is the scene of the book "Island of Disaster" by Lewis Spence. The islands, as are those in the next group, are the breeding ground of the grey seal.

The Monach Isles lay off the coast at Kilmuir. The islands which comprise Shillay (with a disused lighthouse), Ceann Iar and Ceann Ear (joined at low tide), the reefs of Stockay and several isolated rocks are now part of The Nature Conservancy. The islands provide outstanding examples of shell sand habitat and all the essential features of uncultivated machair and shell sand dunes. Additionally they are wintering grounds for barnacle and white-fronted geese and a refuge for wild fowl.

Connected to North Uist by a causeway is Baleshare, a tidal island. Its sister island was engulfed at the same time as Pabbay Sound and Monach Sound were enlarged. Here can be seen an ancient ecclesiastical building called Christ's Temple.

From Benbecula :

Off the east coast of this island are numerous tiny islands with their duns that date back to the first or second century. These same islands were the ones which Prince Charles landed on before approaching Skye.

From South Uist :

Within Loch Druidebeg lay the three hundred and sixty five islands that belong to The Nature Conservancy. As we noted they are the most important breeding ground in Britain for the grey lag goose. A permit is needed to visit the islands during the breeding season; this may be obtained from The

Conservancy. Accommodation is available at a hostel at Grogarry.

Oronsay Island is located off the shores of Daliburgh; it can be approached at low tide. The best time to visit it is in the spring when it becomes a mass of primroses.

Eriskay, as we said, is the first island where Bonnie Prince Charlie landed on the 23rd of June 1745. Much of its fame derives from this and residents will be only too glad to show you the "Prince's Flower" (a pink convulvus which has blossomed every year since his landing) and the "Prince's Strand" (where he stepped ashore and found accommodation at a "mean" hut).

There still remains a good strain of the famous Eriskay pony which is used for carrying peats from the hills, seaweed from the shore and, sometimes, for ploughing. The island's folksongs were immortalised by Marjory Kennedy-Fraser.

In the Sound, in 1941, the S.S. "Politician" foundered with twenty thousand cases of whiskey on board; the incident was made famous by Compton Mackenzie in "Whiskey Galore". The church (Roman Catholic) of St. Michael's is notable for its bell which was recovered from a German battleship sunk in Scapa Flow and for its paintings by John Duncan.

From Eriskay you can visit Stack Island. Here you can see the ruins of the castle that belonged to the pirate Macneil.

Accommodation is available on the island in the form of a guest house and of a cottage croft. However, if you do decide to make your way back to South Uist, note the colonies of seals along the way.

Bus service between North Uist, Benbecula and South Uist is limited and therefore if you plan to use public transport send for (and check) the schedules. If worse come to worse, the local Tourist Offices can fix you up with a taxi, but this might prove to be a rather expensive venture. Tours are sometimes given of the islands, but again you should check at the Tourist Offices for these (see Local Information).

Further information about inter-island services can be obtained from MacBraynes or from The Western Isles Tourist Organisation. "On the spot" boat reservations can also be made locally, but all of these depend upon the tides.

Accommodation

It must be admitted that accommodation on these islands is not as much in abundance as on Lewis and Harris. To be sure there are a few hotels, guest houses, bed and breakfast places, in addition to a few caravans for hire (on the Uists, Berneray and Eriskay). There is a youth hostel located at Howmore on South Uist. Finally, between the three islands there are only two organised camp sites. For an accommodation list write to The Western Isles Tourist Organisation; be sure to book early.

Eating facilities

As with public transport and accommodation, eating facilities are rather limited. There are shops in Lochmaddy, Daliburgh and Lochboisdale (to name a few) and some provision has been made for afternoon tea. Fish, either fresh or cooked, is also available at some ports. If you plan to stay on the islands very long I would suggest that you bring a few "goodies" from the mainland to augment the shops' staples and the evening meal served at your hotel or bed and breakfast place. (The islanders, by the way, never stint on whiskey.)

Sport

The islands have much to offer in the way of sporting facilities.

Fishing and Sea Angling : The preponderance of so many lochs — all of them fish plentiful — has made the islands renowned for salmon and brown trout fishing. Additionally there is a great deal of sea angling, though there is much evidence to suggest that South Uist offers more facilities for this. Cod, haddock, pollack, coalfish, skate, hake, dogfish, conger and tope are in abundance, with the landing of sharks and other predatory fish a distinct possibility. Fishing is, as usual, controlled and permits are required. For details write to The Western Isles Tourist Organisation or Mr David L. Cockburn, Secretary of the North Uist Angling Club, 12 Dunrossil Place, Lochmaddy, Isle of North Uist, and Mr R. T. Sutton, Secretary of the South Uist Angling Association, 13 Liniclate, Benbecula, Isle of South Uist. Additional information can be found in The Scottish Tourist Board's two publications : "Scotland for Fishing" and "Scotland for Sea Angling" (25p and 20p). Remember there is no fishing on Sundays.

Hillwalking and Climbing : Both of the Uists offer much for the hillwalker and climber. Favourite hill walks include Blashaval Hill, Grogarry Mor, Grogarry Beag, Ben Mor, Ben Breac, Sgurra Sollas, Marrival, Ben a' Charra and the Lees in North Uist. The only mountain in North Uist is Mount Eaval which is 1,138 feet. Here you will find a cave and two duns. On Benbecula there is only one hill — Rueval — which is five hundred feet high. On South Uist you can choose from the mountains of Ben More (2,034 feet) and Hekla (1,988 feet) and other minor peaks along the east coast.

Golf : A nine hole golf course is located at Askernish, South Uist. It is reputed to be "a mini version of the classical Scottish sea-side links". Clubs are for hire and the fees are rather low.

Shooting : Shooting is available on South Uist, mainly for snipe, duck and geese. Further information should be obtained from The South Uist Tourist Organisation (see Local Information).

Swimming and Surfing : The west coasts of all the islands are perfect for bathing and swimming; some of the rollers are excellent for surfing.

Places of interest

On North Uist :
Lochmaddy is the principal port of the island and an im-

portant fishing area. It derives its name from the three strangely-shaped basalt rocks at the entrance to the harbour. These are called "maddies" and are in the form of crouching dogs (in Gaelic "madadh" means dog).

A mile from Lochmaddy is Sponish where an important seaweed processing factory is located.

At Ruchdi you can see the home of the late Lord Dunrossil, previously W. S. Morrison, who was for many years Speaker of the House of Commons. He took his title from a hill in the vicinity, Dun Rossil, which is the site of an ancient fort. The house is now occupied by Lord Dunrossil's brother, Dr John Morrison, who is Chief of the Clan Morrison Society.

Nearby, in a shallow loch close to the Newton Ferry Road, is the site of another ancient fort, Dun an Sticir. It is accessible by means of a causeway and is reputed to have been the last inhabited dun in North Uist. From 1601 to 1602 Hugh MacDonald, who laid claim to North Uist, took refuge there to defend himself from the island's real heir. He was betrayed, captured and then taken to Skye where he was imprisoned in the dungeons of Duntuilm Castle. Tradition says he was fed on salt beef until he died of thirst.

One mile down the Newton Ferry Road are the well-preserved ruins of a pre-Reformation Church, dedicated to St. Columba. Locally it is known as Clachan Sands or St. Columba's Churchyard.

An archæological site of some interest is Coileagan an Udal which is about a mile north of Grenitote, Sollas. Here you can see ancient underground wheel houses which were excavated under the auspices of Edinburgh University. At one time a village stood here, but the residents were evicted during the Clearances and their homes were set on fire.

The last sword duel to be fought in North Uist took place at Dunskellor, with Ewen Macdonald of Vallay fighting Macleod of Harris. The referee was Colin Macdonald of Boisdale, who declared Macdonald of Vallay the winner.

On the shore side of the road from Scolpaig stands the Latin Kilpheder Cross which was unearthed from an old cemetery and placed there by Dr Alexander Macleod.

Loch Hosta is reputed to cover the site of a village formerly inhabited by the "Sons of Murdoch" who were at enmity with the "Sons of Gorrie". One night the latter altered the course of a burn which flowed from his loch, engulfing the village and forming the present Loch Hosta.

Close by is Balranald House, belonging to the eldest cadet family of the House of Sleat, the Macdonalds of Griminish.

A natural arch made of rock and a spouting cave — called Kettle Spout — is located on the shore of Tigharry. Here, too, are the Pigeon Caves where hundreds of pigeons nest annually.

Near Hougharry is Ard a' Runair, the birthplace of the most famous of all the Uist Bards — John MacCodrum. Also in the area is Kilmuir Churchyard, the last resting place of the Uist nobility. There are many interesting old tombstones to be seen, among them the flat tombstone with the engraved Macdonald coat of arms, marking the grave of Hugh Macdonald of Baleshare Island. It was Hugh's brother, Donald Roy, who made the arrangements for Bonnie Prince Charlie's escape from Skye.

Clachan is the reputed birthplace of Edward Burke, Prince Charles' faithful servant.

On the slope of Ben Langass and easily accessible from the Lochmaddy to Clachan Road is the chambered cairn of Langash Barp. It is thought to have belonged to the Neolithic Age and to have been the tomb of a famous warrior.

The most conspicuous stone circle in North Uist is called Pobull Fhinn or Fingal's People; it is situated on Ben Langash near Loch Langais.

At Cairnish are two interesting ecclesiastical buildings, Trinity Temple (in Gaelic "Teampull na Trionaid") and McVicar's Temple ("Teampull Clann a Phiocair"). Trinity was founded by Beatrice, daughter of Somerled of the Isles, in 1203 and was later rebuilt by Aimie McRury, the wife of John, First Lord of the Isles. Nearby is the site of a college where chieftains sent their sons to learn Latin and English. Close by this is a battlefield with a ditch called the Ditch of Blood ("Feithe Na Fala"). It was here that the Battle of Carinish took place in 1601, between the Macleods of Harris and the Macdonald's of Uist.

Sixteen miles from Lochmaddy, on the west side of North Uist, are twenty-five acres of bulb land. The bulbs bloom in May and are replaced by gladiolus which are in bloom during July and August.

On Benbecula :

At Stiarvala one can see the remains of a chambered cairn; several of its stones have been removed and there are several ruined shielings built partly on the cairn itself and in its immediate vicinity.

At Balivanich is the site of an old monastery and further down south are the ruins of Borve Castle, once the stronghold of the Benbecula Clan Ranald. Once an island stood opposite, but the machair sands have blown over it and now it is no longer visible.

At Nunton one can see the ruins of the home that belonged to Flora Macdonald's family. It was here that she waited for word that all was ready for her voyage with Prince Charles over to Skye.

The Macdonalds house was once a nunnery, with the buildings dating from the fourteenth century. During the Reformation it was plundered and all the nuns killed. With her dying breath one of them uttered a curse on the island, saying that no priest would ever be born in Benbecula, and this has remained true.

At Rossinish, on the north east coast, Flora Macdonald and Prince Charles sailed for Skye.

On South Uist :

In the village of Eochdar is the South Uist Black House Museum. Among the items to be seen are a hand loom, a pigskin purse given to Flora Macdonald by Prince Charles, and a piece of tartan worn by the Prince when he was in South Uist.

On Reuval Hill or the Hill of Miracles is the imposing statue of the Madonna and Child. Called "Our Lady of the Isles" it was erected in 1957 by the Catholic community with contributions from all over the world. The statue, which is the work of Hew Lorimer, has a face typical of a Uist woman. It is believed to be one of if not the largest religious statues in Scotland.

Legend has it that a woman called Big Margaret prophesied that an army would cover South Uist from the South Ford to the Sound of Eriskay. The islanders, at first, believed this to be true when soldiers over-ran the island, looking for

Bonnie Prince Charlie. However the existence of the Rocket Range, near West Geirnish, might in fact eventually bear this out.

A favourite feeding ground for swans, Loch Bee, is located nearby; as with some of the other long lochs we have seen, it nearly cuts the island in half.

West of Loch an Athain, near Stoneybridge, is the standing stone of An Carra. It is nearly seventeen feet tall and almost triangular in shape.

Barp, a chambered cairn, is located just to the south of Loch Ath Ruaidh, a mile north east of North Frobbost. It is almost circular, measuring seventy-eight feet from north to south, seventy-three feet from east to west, and twelve feet in height.

Howmore is a historic spot on the island and there is much to see in this area. Here you can find the ruins of a church dedicated to St. Columba; its name is Caibeal Dhiarmaid. Sections of the chapel, with traces of a window in the south wall, also remain. There are ruins of Teampull Mor, a church dedicated to St. Mary, and to the south of it there are the remains of its chapel.

At Howmore you can also see the headstone of the grave of the ancient Chiefs of Clan Ranald, while at Ormaclete there are the ruins of another Clan Ranald seat. Ormaclete Castle took seven years to build; however it was only lived in for the succeeding seven years. It was burnt down in 1715 when the venison, being roasted to celebrate the Battle of Sheriffmuir, caught fire. A well-weathered crest and shield of the Clan is over one of the doorways. A third house was eventually built in the southern part of the island but of this little remains.

Across the moors of Howmore is the cave where Prince Charles lived, and from where he made various excursions north as far as Stornoway and as far south as Calvey Island in Lochboisdale, trying to contact the ship to take him back to France. He left the Hebrides on the 26th of June 1746.

Two Roman Catholic Churches, one restored (at Bornish) and the other new (at Garrynamonie) are well worth a visit Also of interest is the Howmore Church of Scotland, one of the only two left in Scotland with a central communion pew.

A cairn at Milton marks the birthplace of Flora Macdonald. All that remains of the house is a low, L-shaped foundation. The circular remains of an earth house ("Uamh Iosal") can still be seen one half mile west of Usinish Bay. There are a number of ruined shielings in the area.

At Kilphedar are the remains of a fine group of wheel houses, late-Iron Age huts with radial partitions.

A seaweed factory is located on the shore near Orasay Island.

Specialised interests

The Uists and Benbecula offer much for those with specialised interests. For the archæologist there are duns, cairns and wheel houses and other ancient remains (see above). Excavations are still at an early stage on these islands, and, to be sure, there is much more to be done.

For the ornithologist and botanist there is a wide range of bird life (eighty species have been sighted) and flora. At Balranald Nature Reserve on North Uist there are forty species alone, including the dabchick, gadwall, wigeon, shoveler, eider, red-breasted merganser, water rail, corncrake and more. The Nature Reserve in the Monach Isles is the wintering ground for white-fronted geese and a refuge for wild fowl. The grey lag goose — in abundance — can be seen at the Nature Reserve on Loch Druidberg. For the botanist there are royal ferns, just a sample of one of the types of flowers that grow on these islands. For additional details contact The Nature Conservancy, 12 Hope Terrace, Edinburgh EH9 2AS, and The Royal Society for the Protection of Birds, 17 Regent Terrace, Edinburgh EH7 5BN.

Further information

Events include : North Uist Highland Games (18th of July in 1972); South Uist Highland Games (19th of July) with the famous piping contests.

Local information

The Western Isles Tourist Organisation, South Beach Quay, Stornoway, Isle of Lewis.

Tourist Information Centre, Lochmaddy Pier, Lochmaddy, Isle of North Uist.

Tourist Information Centre, Lochboisdale, Isle of South Uist.

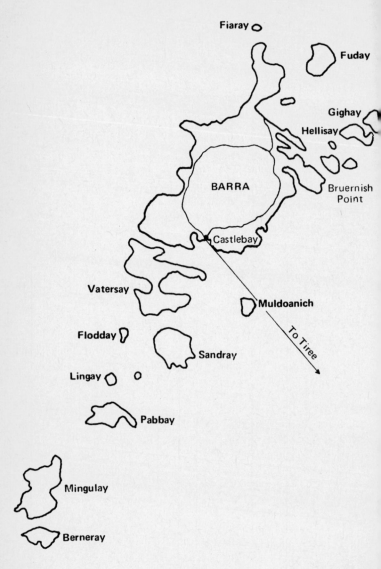

Fiaray

Fuday

Gighay

Hellisay

BARRA

Bruernish
Point

Castlebay

Vatersay

Muldoanich

To Tiree

Flodday

Sandray

Lingay

Pabbay

Mingulay

Berneray

142

BARRA AND THE BARRA ISLES

Description

Situated at the tail end of the "Long Chain" and trailing off into the sea are Barra and a host of lesser isles, including Vatersay, Sandray, Pabbay, Mingulay and Berneray.

Barra is a delightful little island where, because of its size (it is eight miles long and four miles wide), there are scenic changes in very quick succession. Its interior is mainly barren and mountainous, and its entire coastline is deeply indented with bays. There are lovely beaches in the west and cliffs in the east. In the spring and summer it is covered with primroses and wild flowers, earning its name "The Primrose Isle".

Alternatively peaceful and playful, Barra offers the visitor much pleasantness to pass the time away.

For the sportsman and his family there are walks, climbs (Ben Tangaval and Heaval mountains are both over one thousand feet), excellent trout fishing in its recently re-filled lochs and sea angling. Additionally there are many beautiful beaches, bays for swimming and surfing, and even a tennis court !

Places of interest abound, both on the island and its very accessible neighbours. Here, on Barra, you can see the famous Kisimul Castle, the stronghold of the Clan Macneil, which has been recently restored to its previous grandeur by an American architect — the forty-fifth chief of the clan. There are churches as well, with their old graveyards and Celtic remains. Duns, cairns, brochs and standing stones are much in evidence on the island, but because most are un-marked, you, the tourist, can turn archæologist, however briefly.

143

The social life of the islanders is quite intense, with a variety of entertainment being arranged for the evenings. This includes dances, ceilidhs, treasure hunts and fishing competitions.

In spite of its size, the island supports a population of just over 1,200. The mainstay of the island is crofting, but in recent years industries have sprung up on Barra. Now there are factories which turn shell grit into harl for rough-casting houses, which make perfume for export, and which assemble thermostat components for a company manufacturing switches for electric radiators, blankets and kettles.

History

The history of Barra is Hebridean history in miniature. The island is believed to have been named after St. Finbarr of Cork who lived *c.* 550 - 623. Like the other islands in the group it was occupied by Norsemen after the ninth century. When Norway owned Shetland, Orkney, the Hebrides and the Isle of Man in addition to a large part of Ireland, Barra was considered and used as the half-way staging post of the sea route from Bergen to Dublin and Limerick. As with the other islands, Norse place names are in evidence.

Since the Norse invasions Barra has been associated with the Clan Macneil, whose chiefs held it first from the Lords of the Isles. The Macneils were a branch of the Irish O'Neils and the connection with Ireland remained strong for centuries. In the late sixteenth century the people of Barra used to sail to Ireland for religious festivals.

Barra, too, played its part in the Jacobite uprising of 1745 when it was used as a centre for hiding Spanish money and arms landed for the Jacobite army.

In 1747 the Macneils abandoned Kisimul and moved to Eoligarry. Less than one hundred years later they sold the island because of financial adversity to Colonel Gordon of Cluny, who had also purchased South Uist. Colonel Gordon cleared the land, evicted every crofter, and transported much of the island's population to Canada. The survivors grew in number, and in spite of the fact that there was a brief burst of prosperity in the herring industry, they clamoured for land. Squatting began and finally, in 1906, the new owner Lady Gordon Cathcart made a small grant. The furore continued, with many of the squatters being put in prison. In 1937 the greater part of the island was bought back by the late Robert Lister Macneil (father of the present clan chief). The remainder is now owned by the Department of Agriculture and Fisheries for Scotland, who are now in the process of aiding the re-growth of the fishing industry.

How to get there

Barra is serviced by MacBraynes steamers from Mallaig and Oban. During the summer there is a three times weekly car ferry from Mallaig to Castlebay on Barra and a once weekly steamer service from Oban, also docking at Castlebay.
BEA provides a daily service from Glasgow. Planes land at the Cockle Strand ("Traigh Mhor") which is simply a flat beach, washed over twice daily by the tide !

Inter- and intra-island travel

To reach the larger islands in the Outer Hebrides you can either take a MacBraynes steamer or car ferry from Castlebay to Lochboisdale on South Uist, then proceed northwards from there, or you can hire a boat at Eoligarry which will take you to Ludag on South Uist.
MacBraynes also service some of the Inner Hebridean islands from Barra. These include Mull, Coll and Tiree and all of them are reached from Castlebay.
The proximity of the Barra or Bishop's Isles and their many interesting sights provides the visitor with many pleasurable day-trips.
Vatersay is the second largest of the group and the only one that is still populated, though this is very much in decline.

It is virtually two islands, almost crescent shaped, and connected by a narrow belt of dunes. It was here that the squatters first made their land raids. Many of those who went to jail later returned to the island and settled there with honour.

The island contains some lovely beaches, with surfing usually done on the west beach. Here, too, you will find the "Annie Jane" Monument. This marks the shipwreck, in 1853, of the emigrant ship "Annie Jane" which was bound for America from Liverpool, and which sank in the waters off Vatersay.

Vatersay is reached by a small ferry that goes from Castlebay to the pier on Vatersay.

Mingulay — the "Bird Island" — is the third largest in the group, measuring only two miles by one. The island has been deserted since the turn of the century when the land raiders moved onto Vatersay; remains of their old settlement can be seen.

The most important feature of the island is the seven hundred and fifty foot cliff on the south west side which is the home of countless sea birds. The other cliffs range between seven hundred and nine hundred feet, and boats can pass easily between them as their rocks have been fissured by whin dykes which have been washed out by the sea. These are the breeding stations of guillemots, kittiwakes, razorbills and puffins.

In the northern part of the island is a hill called Macphee's Hill, so named for a man who climbed it day after day while waiting for a relief ship from Barra. He had been sent to investigate Mingulay after there was a lapse in communication, and when he arrived he found all the residents dead from the plague. Macphee was therefore forced to spend a year on the island and, when the time was up, he was brought home and, later, given a grant of land.

A day trip to Mingulay — also famed for its boat song — takes place every Sunday during the season.

Berneray is a windy, storm-tossed island. It has been deserted for the last forty years and, like Mingulay, its population consists of birds, many of whom settled there from St. Kilda and North Rona. On Barra Head, the southernmost point in the Outer Hebrides, stands a lighthouse that is visible for thirty-three miles.

Pabbay is noted for its ancient stones, one of which includes a Pictish symbol. There is also an ancient burial mound on the island. Sandray, also deserted, is famed for its abundant flowers.

These islands can be reached from Barra by hired boat.

Additional information about transport can be obtained from MacBraynes, BEA and The Western Isles Tourist Organisation. If you wish to camp on the islands, contact the Tourist Office at Castlebay (address is listed in Local Information).

Barra does not, at present, have any public transport, although the GPO does intend running a twice-daily dormobile from Castlebay to the outlying districts. There are cars and bicycles for hire; however, the best tours are taken by foot.

Accommodation

Accommodation on Barra is, of course, limited. It does have one licensed hotel at Castlebay, three guest houses and many bed and breakfast places. Thirteen croft cottages can also be rented, and there is one caravan for hire. For further information contact The Western Isles Tourist Organisation and the Highlands and Islands Development Board. Need I say book early ?

Eating facilities

As with the other smaller islands, eating facilities are limited. There are a few shops in Castlebay in addition to one or two cafes. Meals can be obtained at the place where you decide to stay. If in doubt, bring food from the mainland.

Sport

Fishing and Sea Angling : As the local lochs have been re-stocked, there is now excellent trout fishing on the island. Details and permits can be obtained from The Secretary,

Barra Angling Club, Castlebay, Isle of Barra.

Sea angling is just becoming popular and competitions are held throughout July and August. Flounder, grey sole, red garnet, haddock, whiting, saithe and mackerel are in abundance. For further information and lists of boat hirers write to the Tourist Office at Castlebay.

Walking, Hillwalking and Climbing : Suggested walks include the entire coastal road, and Garry to Breivig, Ben Tangaval to Tangusdale, Glen Dorcha to Northbay, Cliat to Vaslane Sands past the Cliat Caves and Seal Bay (watch the seals).

For hillwalking and climbing there are Ben Tangaval (1,092 feet) and Heaval (1,260 feet). The view from the latter is spectacular : you can see all of the Barra Isles (to the south) and the Cullin of Skye, the Small Isles and the coast (to the north and east).

Swimming and Surfing : There are beautiful stretches of sand at Tangusdale, Borve, Allasdale and Vaslane. Bathing, swimming and the like are safe there. Surfing is usually done at Traigh Eais. Seal Bay has a rock pool which is ideal for young children. At low tide cockle gathering on the Cockle Strand is a nice pastime.

Tennis: There is a court at Castlebay.

Places of interest

In Castlebay harbour stands Kisimul Castle, the stronghold of the Macneils. It was the present chief's ancestor who refused Noah's hospitality "as he had a boat of his own". Also, when the old chief of the clan finished eating, a herald would mount the great tower and proclaim : "Hear, O ye people and listen, O ye nations. The great Macneil of Barra having finished his meal, the princes of the earth may dine". And it was Rory Macneil, the pirate, who escaped beheading by a rather cheeky reply to a question posed by King James.

The castle itself, newly restored, was originally the work of Hebridean masons. Its tower dates back to 1120 though the bulk of it is typical of late-mediaeval military architecture.

The new clan chief lives in the castle during the summer months when he opens it to the public. It is approached by boat from the shore.

Eoligarry House, in Eoligarry, was the home of the Macneils after the burning of Kisimul Castle. It was built in the eighteenth century.

Also in Eoligarry is Kilbar or St. Barr's Church. Only the ruins can be seen, but in the churchyard there are a number of Celtic or crusader stones. The only runic stone found in the Hebrides was from Kilbar; it is now at the National Museum of Antiquities in Edinburgh.

In the middle of Loch St. Clair are the ruins of a castle, once known as Macleod's Tower. Nearby is St. Columba's Well. At Craighton you can see St. Brendan's Church which was dedicated to the Irish navigator saint who sailed the Atlantic and discovered the "Land of Promise".

On the shoulder of Heaval is an Italian marble Madonna, placed there in 1954. Like South Uist and part of Benbecula, Barra's residents are Catholic.

At Northbay are the ruins of an old mill, used by the people of the southern isles as well as the people of Barra. Each island and each township were allocated a particlar day there each year.

Visit the Hebridean Perfume factory which also displays local craft shell work and polished stones.

Specialised interests

Barra and the Barra Isles are quite popular with archæologists, ornithologists and botanists. Annual expeditions are usually made by naturalists to Mingulay.

Local information

The Western Isles Tourist Organisation, South Beach Quay, Stornoway, Isle of Lewis.
Tourist Office, Castlebay, Isle of Barra.

ST. KILDA

Description

More than one hundred miles west of the Scottish mainland
and forty-five miles west of the Outer Hebrides lay a group
of islands collectively known as St. Kilda. In addition to the
main island, Hirta, the group includes Soay, the sheep isle,
Boreray, the gannet's isle, with its neighbouring stacs, Stac an
Armin and Stac Lee, and Dún, the smallest island, and the
Stac of Levenish. All are owned by The National Trust for
Scotland, leased to The Nature Conservancy, and sub-leased
to the Army who have a missile tracking station on Hirta.

For the ornithologist, botanist, mammologist, archæologist
and geologist the offerings of St. Kilda can only be expressed
in superlatives. The islands have the world's largest colonies
of gannets (on Boreray and the Stacs), the largest and oldest
colonies of fulmars in the British Isles, a vast population of
puffins and a wide variety of flora. The cliffs are among the
highest in Europe, rising to nearly 1,400 feet. St. Kilda has its
own sub-species of wren, the St. Kilda wren, and its own sub-
species of field mouse, the St. Kilda field mouse. The small,
horned Soay sheep are endemic. There are colonies of Leach's
and Storm petrel. There is a thriving seal population. There
are pre-historic remains. There are successions of ruined
villages in Hirta, the last one abandoned by its residents who
were evacuated in 1930. It is now being restored.

For four hundred years, since Dean Monro, a missionary,
visited St. Kilda, the "outside world" has been curious about
this unique group of islands with their staggering scenery,
fascinating animal and plant life, and their once vital social
community. Curiosity (of the best and worst sort) impelled
the Victorian and Edwardian tourists to the islands; the

same, perhaps, is still true today. In a sense it is fortunate that the St. Kildans are no longer there.

History

There is, as Philip Sked of The National Trust for Scotland has written, "a small library on the subject (of St. Kilda), for these islands have always excited the imagination". The "definitive" social history was written by Tom Steel and is entitled "THE LIFE AND DEATH OF ST. KILDA" and to this I refer you for fuller description.

Briefly the history of St. Kilda is the history of the most isolated of the Hebridean islands. Its beginnings, like its name, are debatable, though there is evidence to show that there were pre-historic inhabitants. Later there was a Celtic settlement and, perhaps in the sixth century, a Christianisation of its people. The Norse do not seem to have invaded the islands.

For the better part of their history the islands were held by the Macleods of Macleod of Dunvegan on Skye. How the Macleods gained control is unknown, although legend has it that it was won in a boat race to its shores. Macleod's representative, a Harris man, is reputed to have cut off his hand and thrown it onto the island, thereby "reaching" it first.

For centuries the Hirta islanders' economy was arranged on barter. Each year a "tacksman" who leased the island from the landlord came to claim the rents due to him. In turn the islanders would give him the oils and feathers of sea birds, cattle and a small amount of their agricultural and dairy produce. The tacksman would then supply them with tea, sugar and other necessities.

The defeat of the Jacobites and the consequent breaking up of the clan system did not affect the St. Kildans as the Macleods were mainly an island clan. What did effect them, however, was the change in the social and economic conditions on the mainland. On St. Kilda all was held com-

152

munally and there was no money per se; only a tacksman could deal with this and the days of the tacksman were over.

In the latter part of the eighteenth century the Macleod was forced to sell off great parts of his estate, and St. Kilda passed into the hands of his factor. For the next hundred years it was bought and sold again and again, with the result that the islanders suffered when they had a particularly extortionary landlord.

A semblance of salvation appeared when, in 1871, regular tours were arranged to the island. Heretofore their exports — feathers and the like — had declined as there was no longer any market for them. The tourist trade injected capital into the economy but, as Tom Steel writes, "it led to a decline, both in productivity and the St. Kildans' interest in the traditional aspects of their way of life".

A number of other factors contributed to the death of the island. Cut off from the mainland for nine months a year, the St. Kildans braved disaster unaided. Disease made inroads and, in 1912, they faced starvation because the crops had been bad. In 1913 their radio transmitter which was newly installed broke down. Following this the islands were shelled by the Germans during the First World War. Close to the time that a gun was installed on the island the first family left; others followed. In the 1920s "life became impossible" for the forty remaining people, and when flu struck, four St. Kildans died within a week.

In 1929, after they ran out of flour and sugar, the St. Kildans asked to be evacuated. The government decided it would be cheaper to do this than to support them, and so, on the 29th of August 1930, the St. Kildans left their island. They were re-settled on the coast, with twelve going to Oban and the other twenty-four going to Lochaline. In 1934 the Macleods sold the islands to the fifth Marquis of Bute and from there it became a part of The National Trust for Scotland. How the islanders fared can be summed up in one islander's words about St. Kilda : "It was a far better place".

How to get there

The National Trust for Scotland runs six summer voyages to St. Kilda; a stop-off is made (weather permitting) and then the boat continues on to Canna, North Uist, Harris, Barra and Rum. On one of these a "working party" is set ashore for a week, during which time they work on the restoration of the village on Hirta. For information about these tours write to The Cruise Secretary, The National Trust for Scotland, 5 Charlotte Square, Edinburgh EH2 2DU.

Inter- and intra-island travel

The only approachable island is the tiny island of Dún; at low tide you can practically hop from Hirta.
There is, as one would suppose, no public transport on Hirta. Working parties usually have half days free to explore the island.

Accommodation

The National Trust for Scotland provides accommodation in one of the restored cottages; alternatively you can camp out.

Eating facilities

It would seem that you bring most of your food with you when you arrive. However, the Army has a shop-cum-cafe called — do not smile — the "Puff Inn". Here you can purchase hard and soft drinks, cigarettes, chocolates and, no less, picture postcards and Kodak film. There is a games

154

room, a place for showing films, a television, a sink with hot and cold running water, a lavatory and a shower. There is also medical aid for those who require it.

Sport

One sport that Hirta compels you to take part in is climbing — if only to get a closer look at the bird life. The highest point on Hirta is Conachair which tops 1,296 feet; it is also the highest sheer cliff in the British Isles. The second highest point on the island is Oiseval which is nine hundred feet. As far as heights on the surrounding islands and stacs goes the figures are Boreray, 1,245 feet, Stac an Armin, 627 feet, Stac Lee, 544 feet.

Places of interest

Archæological: Prehistoric remains have been found in the north west part of the island in the area of Glen Mhor. Here you will find the remains of an earth house, the oldest dwelling thus far discovered on the island. Also of interest are the stone coffins which are located seventy feet in front of cottage number nine, and the underground chamber which is situated in a small walled enclosure two hundred feet north of the church.

The island contains a number of mediaeval remains. Calum Mor House, which is situated alongside An t Sruthan, takes its name from the "giant" who reputedly built it in a single day. The house is partly subterranean.

One hundred yards away is the site of Christ's Church which disappeared during the last hundred and fifty years.

Two mediaeval settlements are supposed to have existed in the vicinity of the earth house and Calum Mor and in the northern part of the island, close to the site of the prehistoric settlement.

The village itself is, of course, of much interest. The most modern of the cottages dates from 1860; alongside are byres of the black house type. Lady Grange House is to the south of the cottages, which run from east to west. In the middle of the eighteenth century Lady Grange, wife of the Lord-Justice Clerk of Scotland, proved to be so much of a nuisance to her husband that he banished her to St. Kilda. He later celebrated her death three years before her time was up.

Hundreds of cleits, or storage houses, dot the coast of Hirta. These were hewn of rough stone then roofed with turf; there was a door at one end.

Geological : The rocks of St. Kilda are composed of igneous gabbro, not found on other Hebridean islands. (On Dún you can see the Mistress Stone, a pillar of rock that supports a massive horizontal slab. It was here, by the way, that the young St. Kildans performed balancing feats when they were competing for the hand of a woman. A mile away is the Lover's Stone where similar feats were performed.)

Ornithological : On St. Kilda it is estimated that there are 20,000 pairs of birds, with 6,000 alone on the Conachair Heights. These include puffins, fulmars, gannets (an estimated 40,000 pairs are on Boreray), Leach's and Storm petrel (see these, after midnight, on Carn Mor) and the St. Kilda wren (grey-brown on the upper parts and lighter on the lower, with dark brown flecks). Additionally there are gulls, guillemots and shag — to name a few.

Mammalogical : Here you can see the Soay sheep (in appearance like mountain goats) and the St. Kilda field mouse (with a reddish-brown back and yellow underparts).

Botanical : Hirta is particularly lush and here you can see primroses, roseroot and even honeysuckle on the cliffs.

Local information

The National Trust for Scotland, 5 Charlotte Square, Edinburgh EH2 2DU.

The Nature Conservancy, 12 Hope Terrace, Edinburgh EH9 2AS.

The Royal Society for the Protection of Birds, 17 Regent Terrace, Edinburgh EH7 5BN.